STORIES FROM THE DARK NIGHT

STORIES FROM THE DARK NIGHT

WRITING AS A TOOL FOR GRIEF

KAREN WYATT MD

Stories from the Dark Night

Writing as a Tool for Grief

by Karen Wyatt

Published by Sunroom Studios

Silverthorne, CO 80498

Copyright © 2023 by Karen M. Wyatt, MD

Illustration by Larry George

All rights reserved, including the right of reproduction in whole or in part in any form.

ebook ISBN: 979-8-9861488-6-1

Paperback ISBN: 979-8-9861488-7-8

Printed in the United States of America

*This book is dedicated to Larry, Aaron and Gia.
May you always hear the meadowlark sing.*

Illustration by Larry George, MD

The child whispered, "God, speak to me." And a meadowlark sang but the child did not hear.
So the child yelled, "God, speak to me!" And the thunder rolled across the sky but the child did not listen.
The child looked around and said, "God, let me see you!" And a star shone brightly but the child did not notice.
And the child shouted, "God, show me a miracle!" And a life was born but the child did not know.
So the child cried out in despair, "Touch me God, and let me know you are here!" Whereupon God reached down and touched the child.
But the child brushed the butterfly away and walked away unknowingly.

— Ravindra Kumar Karnani

CONTENTS

Introduction   xi

PART I
WRITING OUR GRIEF

1. Writing Our Grief   3

PART II
FIND A LIFELINE

2. Find a Lifeline   11
3. Griefwork   15
4. Stick and Rock   17
5. Silver Maple Leaf: A Short Story   21

PART III
REPAIR THE FOUNDATION

6. Repair the Foundation   31
7. The Perfect Mother   35
8. Mother and Child   41
9. Fathers: Good and Bad   43
10. If You Really Loved Me ...   47

PART IV
DISCOVER MEANING

11. Discover Meaning   51
12. Why Me?   55
13. To What Purpose Have I Been Brought   61
14. Lessons from Peeling Apples   65
15. Grief and the Garden   69

PART V
RECOGNIZE THE DIVINE

16. Recognize the Divine   73
17. What You See is What You Get   75

18. Finding Maria	81
19. Katya's Trees	85
A Fable About Life and Death	

PART VI
OPEN TO COMPASSION

20. Open to Compassion	97
21. A Mother's Healing Love	99
22. Brian's Last Run	103
23. Love Needs No Words	107
24. Sixty Miles to Paradise	111

PART VII
UNEARTH THE TRUTH

25. Unearth the Truth	123
26. Meadowlark	125
27. Shattered	131

PART VIII
CLEANSE THE SOUL

28. Cleanse the Soul	135
29. A Hint of Old Spice	137
30. Cave Bath	139

PART IX
BE AT PEACE

31. Be at Peace	149
32. When Doctors Grieve	151
33. Another Hollyhock Miracle	155
34. Blessed are Those Who Mourn	157
35. Something from Nothing	161
A Path Through Grief	
36. Falling Trees	167
About the Author	175
Also by Karen Wyatt MD	177

INTRODUCTION

Stories have played an integral role in our existence since the dawn of Man. Conveying culture, history, meaning, identity, and faith, stories connect us with all of mankind across time and beyond all societal barriers; and our stories also set us apart. Just as humans are the only living creatures on this planet who are aware of our own mortality, we are also the only beings, to our knowledge, who tell stories to inspire and teach one another. In fact, stories have the potential to be a more powerful teaching tool than lectures or discourse, because they touch the heart and soul as well as the mind.

In my own family history, stories have been an important means of communication and entertainment. My father, though shy and often quiet-spoken, was a wonderful storyteller, as was his father. Dad could captivate us with his tales of herding sheep in the Bighorn Mountains when he was a boy, his adventures as a soldier during World War II and humorous depictions of the colorful old ranchers he had gotten to know through the years. Like Dad and Grandpa, from the time I was very young, I seemed to view everything that happened around me as a story. This particular way of viewing life helps add meaning and resolution to the seemingly random and senseless events that unfold around us. There is a certain comfort in being able to see the themes, plots and patterns of this universe and in setting them down in words for others to share and enjoy.

As a physician, I utilize stories to help patients see their own lives from a different perspective and to share the wisdom I have learned by observing the lives and struggles of others. And, when I myself needed to heal after my father's death, I wrote story after story to help me put the pieces back together and find a way to carry on. Writing was my lifeline as I coped with a dark night that seemed never-ending. I wrote from within the darkness of grief rather than about grief itself.

The following stories and poems from my collection provide an anthology of my process of learning to live with traumatic grief. They represent the rough and faltering path I have followed for three decades since my father's suicide. Some of them, like *Stick and Rock* and *If You Really Loved Me* were written in response to prompts from my writing teachers.

While the healing process differs for every individual, I offer these stories that have saved my life, in hopes that others may find guidance or comfort in the lessons they provide. Each section includes a few writing prompts in case you too would like to use writing as a tool for grief.

PART I

WRITING OUR GRIEF

1

WRITING OUR GRIEF

"Give sorrow words; the grief that does not speak knits up the o'er-wrought heart and bids it break."

— WILLIAM SHAKESPEARE

Since ancient times humans have used words to express their grief. From the lamentations of ancient Egyptians to Medieval death poetry to combat diaries from World War II to contemporary grief memoirs like *The Year of Magical Thinking* by Joan Didion and *Wild* by Cheryl Strayed, we write to "give sorrow words," release our pain, and hopefully to make sense of the world again.

For me, during the years after my father's death by suicide, writing was my salvation, providing an outlet for all of the troubling emotions that welled up inside, a distraction from the hopelessness that haunted me, and a channel for the flow of creative life energy that helped me hold on. I was lost in the "dark night" for many years, barely able to glimpse the stars and the moon that were struggling to show me my path. But writing gave me a way to gradually, ever so slowly, return to the light.

Benefits of Writing for Grief

Studies have shown numerous benefits from writing about grief and other difficult experiences. The practice of "expressive writing," where our deepest emotions and thoughts are explored on paper for just 15 minutes per day, can lead to decreased anxiety and depression. Writing about grief helps validate our experience and release our repressed thoughts and feelings. We can also reflect on our own pain more easily in the form of written words, which allows us to gain a new perspective on our situation.

Writing during a time of chaos can help us find structure and create meaning from our pain. We can also record memories that help us form continuing bonds with our loved one and can be revisited over time. Composing a letter to a deceased loved one provides a place to finally say all the things we neglected to say when they were alive.

When we write in our own journal we create a safe space where anything and everything can be shared—even those thoughts and feelings that we fear no one else will understand. We may discover insights and clarity through our own words that were hidden from view before. Symbols and patterns may emerge in our writing that can lead us to deeper opportunities for healing.

Types of Writing to Consider

Freeform writing in a journal can provide an outlet for emotions and help you express things that you find difficult to talk about. Write quickly whatever comes to mind without judging or questioning yourself. Don't worry about spelling or grammar, just record the words that arise in the moment. As mentioned above, studies show that this type of expressive writing for just 15 minutes per day is beneficial, especially if you explore your deep emotions.

Writing letters to the person who died or to yourself can be an effective way of addressing unspoken issues from the past. You can say what you never dared to say when that person was alive, whether positive or negative, and find some relief in finally speaking your truth.

Poetry can be a wonderful way to write about grief through symbols and creative language. Even if you've never written a poem before you may find that your emotions are best conveyed in brief phrases and descriptive words. If a poem comes through you unexpectedly (as it did for me) don't judge, just record the words and let it speak it's own message.

Guided writing prompts may be helpful on days when you feel you have no words of your own to express. Prompts are an indirect form of inspiration that get you started with a particular idea. From that point the flow may open and you may end up at a very different place from where you started. This book includes some writing prompts for each section that may serve you when your own well runs dry.

Fictional stories are also an indirect way of writing about your grief. They allow you to get perspective on your own experience and to create characters who may be very different from you. By entering the emotional world of your characters you have a chance to envision the healing and growth that may seem elusive to you in real life.

Memoir writing allows you to tell the story of your own process of grief and can be therapeutic as you review your past loss and all of the ups and downs of your journey. This form of writing allows you to see your history from a higher perspective and to share the insights and wisdom you've gained over time. Memoirs are usually best written after a significant amount of time has passed to allow your long-term vision to develop.

My Grief Writing

In this book you'll find examples of most of the types of writing listed above. Early in my grief experience I primarily did freeform writing in my private journal and I haven't shared much of that here, but my journaling practice eventually opened the channel for other forms of writing.

Though I am not a poet I found that spontaneous poems arose on the pages of my journal from time to time. They usually expressed something I couldn't seem to say in plain prose and often surprised me with their raw honesty. But they proved to be of great value to me as I returned to them again and again, always finding new and deeper meaning there.

During my years of grief I attended several writing workshops where no one knew I was grieving. The guided prompts I received there were very helpful to inspire me to write about other things, even though my grief was often hidden inside the words. I've included some of the pieces I wrote for those workshops so you can see the benefit of using prompts to broaden your writing.

Over the years of my grieving I began to envision a number of fictional stories that I longed to tell (and still do.) Two of them found their way into this book, *Silver Maple Leaf* and *Katya's Trees*, both of which were enjoyable and cathartic to write. Now my brain is crowded with many more stories because I'm no longer occupying so much bandwidth with ruminations on my grief.

Finally, many years into my journey I had gained enough healing and perspective that I could finally write the narrative of my own grief, including stories from my work as a doctor. Since these writings are mostly in chronological order, you will see that the content of my writing shifted over the years. From being unable to write directly about my father's suicide, I was eventually able to write about death, grief, suicide, guilt, my father, and all the pain that I have carried for these many years.

Your Grief Writing

Dear reader, I don't know if writing will be helpful to you in your grief, but if it sounds interesting it's worth giving it a try. I recommend you begin, as I did, with unstructured writing in a journal or diary. Let your thoughts flow freely and uncensored, keep it private, and allow anything and everything to be expressed on paper that comes up for you.

On days when you feel dry and empty inside, try using a writing prompt (such as the ones in this book or from other sources online) or write a letter to yourself or your loved one. Again free yourself from judgment and criticism and let your words speak for themselves.

You may find it helpful from time to time to re-read what you've written in the past, but it's not necessary. Sometimes it's better to just keep going and move on to the next topic or the next journal page.

Even though I've divided my own writing into various parts, there's no real structure or path through this grief journey. So have no expectations or plans for where your writing will take you. Let it be a new experience each time you put pen to paper and trust that somehow the grief you are carrying is doing what it needs to do.

Remember that you are writing from *within* grief rather than writing *about* grief. Your grief has its own messages to share and it will guide and shape what you write over time. Finding the patterns and symbols expressed by your grief is a wondrous part of this writing exploration.

My own journey has taken decades to this point, so please

give yourself all the time you need. Let your writing evolve over months and years and show you how you are changing, growing and healing, but don't try to rush the process.

Author Anne Lamott wrote about her own path of grief:

> "Only grieving can heal grief; the passage of time will lessen the acuteness, but time alone, without the direct experience of grief, will not heal it."

Writing while you are in the midst of grief is an excellent tool for grieving, no matter what you write about. Writing allows you to experience, in a safe space, all of the deep and wide and terrifying and amazing and heartbreaking aspects of your own beautiful grief. May the words you need to write come through on paper and light the way inside your own dark night.

PART II
FIND A LIFELINE

2

FIND A LIFELINE

"Where you used to be, there is a hole in the world, which I find myself constantly walking around in the daytime, and falling into at night."

— Edna St. Vincent Millay

Those initial days after experiencing personal loss or the tragic death of a loved one are filled with confusion, numbness and shock, interrupted by brief slashes of deep, jarring pain like you have never felt before. Over and over you sink into a state of dazed denial about the trauma that has just taken place, only to be shaken awake, repeatedly, by the memory of the exact moment the loss occurred. Nothing seems real anymore and you have no idea how to find your way back to reality.

But, there will be, somewhere hidden in the turbulence and anguish of your early grief, a small miracle; a lyric from a song; even a rock or a leaf; a sign that you are not alone; a lifeline that can sustain you. Hold onto it tightly, even though you don't understand it or know its source. You are going to need help for many months and possibly years and this lifeline will be there for you in the difficult times. Someday, far in the future, it will all make sense to you as the truth is gradually revealed.

You may not be able to speak about the trauma or death or seek support from other people until some of the raw pain heals. You may withdraw into yourself as you struggle just to get through each day. Perhaps you will survive by burying all emotion in order to avoid the pain. This state can last a long time and in the beginning will provide you with life-saving relief from your suffering.

Eventually, however, you will be pushed to grow, to move beyond this place of no feeling. This is when the work will begin. Opportunities will be offered to you to stretch your boundaries, to rise to a place of greater wisdom and to delve deeply into your own soul. When you respond to the call, you will begin to grow, which is ultimately what will heal your devastation.

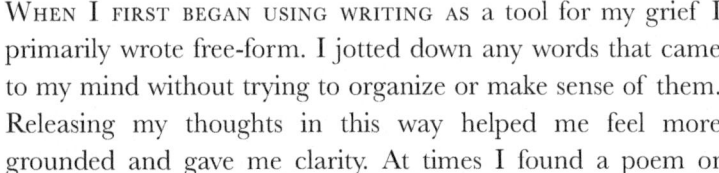

WHEN I FIRST BEGAN USING WRITING AS a tool for my grief I primarily wrote free-form. I jotted down any words that came to my mind without trying to organize or make sense of them. Releasing my thoughts in this way helped me feel more grounded and gave me clarity. At times I found a poem or verse coming through, such as *Griefwork*.

Writing prompts helped release my creativity and reveal some of my repressed pain. On one occasion my writing teacher suggested telling one story from the perspectives of two different people and *Silver Maple Leaf* emerged, to my great surprise.

Writing Prompts:

1. What lifelines are helping you stay afloat right now?
2. What small events trigger your memories and your grief?
3. What story is waiting to be told?

3

GRIEFWORK

Your death goes with me wherever I go.
I find grief in surprising places:
shoved in my pocket
like a forgotten five-dollar bill in last winter's jacket;
or at the back of the closet,
buried under piles of abandoned shoes and clothing.
Discovering this hidden grief
brings not the delight of unearthing a treasure....
but it is, nonetheless,
a gift.
A gift that helps me
wring out my heart once more
and relive the pain,
the questions,
the unknown.
I am working through this grief
like a patchwork quilt.
Each scrap or remnant I find
gets washed by tears,
dried in the sun,

and then mended and sewn together
to make a larger piece
to add to a still larger piece.
The threads I use to sew my grief patches
come from the present,
from living my life
each moment,
fleeting moments like
seeing the sunrise,
a hug from my children,
a certain verse in a song on the radio.
Now my life,
shattered by your death,
has come down to this:
finding enough thread
every day
for the mending.

4

STICK AND ROCK

Assembled before me are two rocks and a stick, intended to inspire my creativity. I am participating in a writing class and my assignment for the week is to find an ordinary object from nature and study it, reflecting upon its ordinariness and attempting to see beauty in its presence.

I have "borrowed" the rocks and the stick from my son's vast "Nature Collection" which sprawls across the top of his dresser. Recalling his habits of picking up random stones and other "treasures" on our outdoor hikes each summer, I am sure that I have seen quite ordinary objects find their way into his pockets and, eventually, onto the dresser-top. This assignment should be easy.

The first stone I have picked to study is smooth and flat and dark grey.

"Rather nondescript," I'm thinking.

But, on closer look, I find that its surface is covered with very tiny, fine pits, as if pricked multiple times with the tip of a pin. The depressions are so small that they can be appreciated only by careful inspection. The surface feels perfectly smooth to my touch. I realize that centuries of weather and physical stress have worn away the tiny fragments of softer stone that had filled each minute crater at some time in its life.

Well ... clearly this is no ordinary rock. In fact, its beauty awes me. I close my eyes and then look again, trying to see ordinariness, but I fail. I simply cannot use this rock for this exercise.

The next rock is much larger and even more ordinary at first glance. It is lighter grey in color and has an irregular oblong shape with a rougher, less appealing surface. Here we go. But, wait ... look at those tiny sedimentary lines running through the entire rock. I could not see their subtle color difference until I got closer. And, on the undersurface of the rock I find something even more amazing. Tiny lazulite flecks appear here and there, suspended in a matrix of uniform greyness like the first stars becoming visible in the night sky.

Incredible. Not ordinary at all.

I realize that I will not be able to find an ordinary rock for this exercise. It is the way I see rocks. Somewhere on the path between mountain and dust particle, each rock at once possesses the singularity of a majestic lofty peak, and the ubiquity of a billion grains of sand. Holding a rock in my hand, I am touching the beginnings of this planet and imprinting my own mark, which will remain until the end of time.

How could I experience this and not recognize beauty? How, indeed.

Only the stick remains to be my ordinary inspiration. But I can already tell that it is a futile exercise. This particular twig, from an old oak tree, has had much of its bark worn away to reveal smooth wood underneath. Several knots form faces along the length of the branch and I notice a healed scar distorting its shape in one area. The bark that remains has a cracked and grooved surface, dry and brittle from prolonged absence of water. I see a pattern of dark and light brown coloration in the bark that is repeated in the wood itself, forming a fine rich grain.

Beautiful. I can find nothing ordinary about this stick. It is the way I see sticks. Time and the elements have made this once supple stalk a sturdy implement for building and burning. This source of nourishment for animal life becomes, in its demise, a means of shelter and warmth. Each branch, each twig, somewhere on a path between acorn and cinder, is so utterly simple and so elegantly significant to all of life.

I'm discouraged now. How will I complete this writing exercise if I cannot find something ordinary to study?

Taking a break to get a glass of water, I catch the reflection of my own face in the kitchen window. Ahhh ... this is where I see ordinariness. Squeezing my eyes closed and then opening them suddenly, again I fail to find beauty in this reflection. It is the way I see myself. It is the way I have always seen myself.

Stars, rocks, mountains, sand, acorns, trees, leaves, sticks ... these have whispered to me the meaning of Beauty since I was a child. And I have been the observer, gazing upon, but never connected to, the beauty I saw around me.

Today I hold the rock and stick to my face. Fine lines etch the tissue around my eyes, forming a rich grain, marking the passage of time. My skin, smooth to the touch, is pitted with deep pores and acne scars, tiny craters left behind after the wearing down by the elements.

Stick and rock. I touch my face and stare at the glass. Perhaps, on this day, a new way of seeing myself will be born within me. Somewhere on my journey from embryo to Spirit, holding every mountain and tree in one hand and reaching toward the stars with the other, I can laugh ... I can sing ... and I can cry.

How can I keep from seeing the Beauty?

5

SILVER MAPLE LEAF: A SHORT STORY

Part 1: Abby

It was 10:45 pm on a Sunday night ... just 15 minutes before Abby Slade should have been going home for the night. But at that moment a call came in from paramedics – they were two minutes out with a hit-and- run victim; auto-pedestrian; multiple trauma. As the intern on the Emergency Room rotation, Abby was required to stay until all patients who came in on her shift were stabilized. She sighed a weary exhalation, knowing that a multiple trauma case could keep her there all night. She grabbed a handful of stale popcorn from the nurses' desk and headed toward the trauma room as the sound of sirens reached a peak.

Suddenly the entire scene shifted into action as the paramedics wheeled in the patient, performing CPR and shouting "Full arrest, one minute ago. He's got blunt trauma to the head and abdomen, bilateral fractured femurs, blown right pupil. We're losing him!"

Immediately, Abby acted and called out orders, though the seasoned ER nurses and techs had carried out her commands before she could even think of what to do next. "Run D5LR full out; amp of bicarb, amp of epi; prepare to defibrillate."

The shock from the paddles against his chest jolted the man's body and silenced the room for a millisecond. Every eye was on the heart monitor ... flat line. Again the team began the same routine: CPR, blood gases, epi and bicarb, defibrillate.

While all of these steps were being taken mechanically, mindlessly, Abby became aware of an undertone in the room. Murmurings of disgust and displeasure: "He's filthy!"

"I'm not touching his shirt."

"Cops say he's a transient, lives on the streets."

Abby was aware of a growing sense of futility in the room as each resuscitation attempt failed. Attention was being focused on her as the person with the authority to decide whether to continue the code or call it quits. This was the moment she had most dreaded in her young medical career. It seemed so simple to all the others in the room to just say, "Stop." And to them it was so obvious that it was the right thing to do.

But, she could not quell the uncertain and anxious thoughts that were rising within her. "How do you know for sure he won't come back? What if his heart would respond if we tried just one more time?"

Some of her hesitation was normal for a new intern—experience is a great teacher for doctors required to make life and death decisions. But, Abby was grappling with a deeper anguish: a memory that had haunted her since she was 12 years old.

Her own father had suffered multiple, severe injuries in an accident and died in an emergency room after a failed resuscitation attempt. For all these years she had questioned the wisdom of the medical staff on call that day: had they really done everything to try to save him? Had they given him a chance or had they simply given up when they got tired?

Her decision to become a doctor had been fueled by her determination that she would not get tired, she would never give up on a patient. But, now, here she was, the staff surrounding her, fatigued from a long day, looking at her expectantly as they went through the routine over and over again. Finally, she took a deep breath and gave the order, "Stop."

As quickly as the action had erupted earlier, silence now engulfed the room. IV's and monitors were removed, tubes vanished, and the staff members sat quietly at their desks, charting a record of the incident. Abby completed her own note efficiently and succinctly, displaying none of the emotion that still tightened her throat. Avoiding notice by the rest of the ER staff, she slipped behind the curtain into the cubicle that housed the lifeless body of the injured man.

Questions and doubts were still swirling in her mind as she pulled the sheet up from under his feet. His body not yet stiff with rigor mortis, Abby moved his right arm and placed it across his chest, noticing the orange hospital armband that encircled his wrist. "John Doe" was inscribed on the band, indicating that he was one of the lost, homeless individuals who huddled in alleys and doorways downtown or under the bridge that crosses the river.

She knew there would be no mourners arriving at the ER, grieving for this John Doe; there would be no obituary in the paper; no funeral where his life would be celebrated and memorialized. His body would be placed in the morgue until the county approved a pauper's burial, which would probably consist of cremation and burial of his ashes.

"Did I do enough?" Abby silently questioned herself.

As she released his right arm and reached for the other, she noticed that his left hand was tightly clenched, holding some small object. Uncurling his fingers and looking more closely, Abby saw within his hand a single, star-shaped leaf. Abby gasped, recognizing instantly that it was a leaf from a silver maple tree, familiar to her because a huge, stately maple had grown in the backyard of her childhood home.

As her finger brushed the velvety silver undersurface of the leaf, she was flooded with memories: climbing that enormous tree while her father looked on, encouraging her to go a little higher, always ready to catch her if she slipped; having "tea parties" with her dolls under the shady arbor of the maple tree's broad branches; and, after her father's death, retreating to the highest limbs of the tree to cry alone while she held tightly to the branch that supported her.

This leaf was like a message from the past, a sign from her father, perhaps, that he was still watching over her, ready to catch her if she slipped. She brushed a tear from her eye as she studied John Doe's face, pale and waxy, yet, at the same time, peaceful and serene. She wondered, though she knew she would never have the answer, "Why was he holding this leaf so tightly? What was his story?"

Suddenly, her reverie was interrupted as her pager sounded, instructing her to call the nurses' station. Abby pressed the leaf into the back of her notebook, then whispered a quiet "Thank you," to John Doe for bringing this small gift to her.

She had survived her first life and death situation as a physician and was aware that some of her anxiety had dissipated. Perhaps she would be able to heal her old grief, after all.

As she turned to leave she looked back one more time and uttered a simple prayer, the only eulogy this patient would receive, "John Doe, may you rest peacefully in the arms of angels, knowing that, for these few moments, you made a difference to someone else."

Part 2: Ben

Ben pulled his worn overcoat a little tighter around him and adjusted the cardboard box he was using to shield himself from the wind. It was a cold and rainy fall evening and he had found a place to settle in early, hoping to get a little sleep. He could smell the aroma of popcorn from the theatre behind him as he huddled against a garbage can in the alley.

Actually, Ben was not his real name. Some of the other drifters down by the tracks had started calling him that when he first came to this town. An old, grey-haired Black man, known as Slats, who lived down near the river and spent his days by the drifters' campfire, had given that name to him.

When the new man first appeared around the campfire, Slats has asked, "Who you be?"

"Nobody," was the reply.

"Well, where you been?"

And the younger man had replied, "Don't know; don't care. I just been."

Slats had laughed, slapped his knee, and said "Jus' been. I'll call you 'Jus' Ben,' how bout that."

From then on the nickname stuck and no one ever again asked the man for his given name. He didn't care. He liked not having a past, not being known by people. He was a loner and wanted it that way. He worked hard at keeping the details of his past out of his thoughts. If he let himself wander into those days he would see in his mind's eye the face of a woman he still loved and a child who must be grown by now ... and the anguish of his loneliness would stagger him with its force.

He focused his thoughts and energy on the moment—where to get a little food, where to sleep, where to go when it rains. He was not unhappy with this life, but, then again, he didn't have any idea what it would mean to be happy. He was without feeling, without roots or ties; he was 'Jus' Ben.'

On this particular Sunday, though, something unusual had happened to Ben. He had been walking down by the river, searching a picnic area for lost change or discarded treasure, when he heard a sound more beautiful than he could ever imagine.

"Angels," he whispered.

He followed the sound across the river to a tiny wooden church, badly in need of paint and repairs. It was the All Souls Baptist Church and the gospel choir was singing and clapping until the entire church building seemed to sway with their heavenly rhythm. As he listened to this beautiful sound, his eye caught something else: a big, old silver maple tree that stood behind the church. It had sturdy low branches and delicate upper limbs that reached to the sky. Most of its leaves had fallen, but a few stalwarts were still clinging tenaciously to tiny twigs.

He climbed up into the strong arms of the tree where he suddenly remembered being eight years old, sitting in the silver maple in his grandmother's yard: safe, protected by the branches, cradled and rocked by the wind. For some time he stayed in that silver maple tree, listening to the heavenly choir sing, while childhood memories flooded him: his parents arguing, his grandma laughing, his little brother crying.

He stayed there until the music had long ceased, the church had emptied, and the rain had started to fall. As he climbed back down, he plucked a single leaf from the tree and placed it in his pocket.

Later that same night, a policeman walking past the Rialto Theatre saw an old bum huddled in the alley under a piece of cardboard. He yelled to the man and told him to move on. Ben wearily stood up and shuffled off down the street. He placed his numb hands into his pockets for warmth and discovered the silver maple leaf he had picked earlier in the day. He felt the velvety smoothness of its silver undersurface and traced the veins with his finger.

Suddenly, a gust of wind stirred and lifted the leaf right out of his hand. He followed its path into the street, determined to retrieve that leaf, not knowing why or what motivated him, only that it felt like getting that leaf back would be the most important thing he had ever done.

And there it was, resting on the asphalt. If he could just jump to it before the wind picked it up again. He took a leap into the street and barely reached the leaf with his left hand as he heard a terrible screeching of tires and a honking horn ... and he saw a light ... a very bright light.

As everything around him faded into blackness, Ben could once again hear the angels singing as he clutched that precious silver maple leaf in his hand.

PART III

REPAIR THE FOUNDATION

6

REPAIR THE FOUNDATION

"It has been said, 'time heals all wounds.' I do not
 agree. The wounds remain. In time, the mind,
 protecting its sanity, covers them with scar tissue
 and the pain lessens. But it is never gone."

— Rose Fitzgerald Kennedy

Before you can proceed with the task of healing your grief from traumatic loss, you must seek to repair the very foundation of your existence—your relationship with your parents. Whether they are living or have passed on, whether they were close or absent during your childhood and whether they were healthy or damaged, your parents have inflicted certain wounds upon your psyche. Now is the time you must find forgiveness and acceptance in your heart in order to move on with the rest of your important work.

∼

WHILE MY FATHER'S suicide death thrust me into a vortex of pain and guilt, I found it relatively easy to find compassion for him. We were so much alike in our temperament and mannerisms that I could "see" him and I could manage the wounds of my childhood.

But my relationship with my mother had been filled with tension, resentment, confusion, and rejection. I couldn't fathom the workings of her mind or her heart. An emotional chasm kept us apart and I was unable to navigate it. As I contemplated my grief over Dad's death I was pulled over and over again toward the insurmountable task of making peace with her. This section contains my attempts to make sense through writing about my raw and fractured relationship with my mother. But I barely touched the surface of the wounds that I would one day explore much more deeply as I cared for her at the time of her death. That story remains to be told.

Grief provides an opportunity to heal the past, even though it requires some of life's most difficult work. But some parents have been toxic and destructive. Some children have struggled to survive the abuse. Working toward forgiveness and healing may not make sense if you are carrying such pain. This will be a long and precarious journey. Some foundations cannot and should not be repaired.

My writing reflects my own path and it may not resonate with your experience. Tell your own story in any way you can; express all of your emotions without shame. Take it slowly, let it come to you gradually, one word or paragraph at a time.

Writing Prompts:

1. Write about a wound that still needs to be healed from your mother and from your father.

2. What are the ways in which your parents have been "perfect" for you? Have any of their flaws helped you grow?
3. What pain do you carry with you from the past?

7
THE PERFECT MOTHER

You may not have given it much thought, but having a loving relationship with your mother is good for your health. Though I make that statement with conviction, I must confess that I am basing it solely on my own non-scientific observations rather than actual data. While I have not read many studies that have specifically analyzed the mother-child relationship in terms of its effect on physical health, I have dissected many life stories in my years of practicing medicine. I have witnessed firsthand many hearts that have been strangled by resentment and a lack of forgiveness toward mothers. From these experiences I have concluded that our mothers, and our ability or inability to love them, figure heavily in our unfolding as healthy beings.

While perusing a local card shop recently, looking for just the right sentiment to send to my own mom for Mother's Day, I noted that there seem to be two varieties of cards for this occasion. There are the somewhat vague and ambivalent "I love you, have a nice day" cards and the sentimental and specific "You are the perfect mother because ..." cards. I personally have never felt quite satisfied with either choice, wishing for one that said, "You weren't perfect but I appreciate how hard you tried." It seemed to me, in the shop that day, that the "Have a nice day" cards outnumbered the "Perfect mother" cards about two to one. Apparently there's a shortage of perfect mothers out there.

Your mother is the first person you ever trusted, the first person you were connected to, and the first person to disappoint you. Your first psychological wounds, as a matter of course, were most likely inflicted by your mother. For, that is the nature of the mother-child relationship. A mother is called to make sacrifices, continually presented with choices whether to soothe her own aching neediness or to surrender her longings for the good of her child.

Some mothers, because of their own deep wounds and failure to grow, find it impossible to make the sacrifices so desperately needed by their children. While some mothers are able to let go of their own selfishness with grace and joy as they care for their children, many others struggle at times with the balance between meeting their own needs and the needs of their offspring. And some mothers suffer disappointment and even resentment during the parenting process, leaving their children to grow up also feeling disappointment and resentment. This, once again, is the nature of the mother-child relationship.

On my own path of motherhood, while I have sought to be the best parent I could imagine, I have had to recognize, quite painfully, that it is not possible to be the perfect mother I always envisioned. Quite unintentionally, I have at times harmed my own children, even while I have worked hard to prevent that from happening. My own wounds have created wounds for them and I have not been able to stop that process, for it is somehow an essential component of our human development.

So, how do we come to terms with our mothers and these

wounds we are left to soothe? The heart thrives on resolution and the mending of those places that have been torn. Our wellbeing soars when broken threads are tied together, when shattered fragments are realigned. For these reasons, it is in our best interest to focus on healing our mother wounds.

This type of healing comes about with our willingness to view the past in a new way, to see what has not been recognized before. In order to heal your relationship with your mother, you must begin to see that even the most careless and selfish mother has made sacrifices in order to give life to her child. From forfeiting her flat belly and firm breasts to losing sleep at night, she has, at the very least, relinquished herself physically in the process of giving birth. Imagine what else she might have left behind in her transition from young woman to mother: her dreams and plans, her own growth as a person, her uniqueness.

You must become aware of all the little sacrifices your mother made, that you could not before appreciate: the books she never read, the dinners that went uneaten, the walks not taken, sweaters not knitted, movies not seen, poems not written, the phone calls cut short, vacations abandoned, naps interrupted. These small things that she gave up and that, most likely, went unnoticed by you, are the essence of her love for you and her devotion to motherhood.

Of course, she wasn't perfect. But, her very flaws and shortcomings, it turns out, were exactly what you needed in order to provide you with wounds from which to grow. For, the rough and painful places in our lives become the catalysts for our eventual spiritual transformation. You must begin to see all of this in a new way, from a new perspective.

Once, at a time in my life, when I was struggling to accept my own parents for who they were and the life they had given me, I had a very powerful dream that changed everything for me. In the dream, I was shown a huge mural, a collage of many, many pictures. As I looked closely, I saw that each picture was a different scene from my life—representing both significant and trivial events, times of celebration and suffering, achievement and failure. I observed that each scene had its own shape and that all of the scenes fit together precisely, as do the pieces of a jigsaw puzzle.

"It's all perfect," I said, recognizing that each event was necessary in order for the picture to be complete.

And my parents —whose presence was a factor in nearly every scene —were also perfect, bringing me exactly the lessons and love and pain that I needed in order to become who I am.

Some years later, in another very symbolic dream, I faced both my parents with love, offering them some sparkling gold dust I was holding in my hands. It was a gesture of forgiveness and acceptance. And when I looked more closely at Mom and Dad, I saw each of their parents standing behind them, awaiting the same gift of golden forgiveness; and then I saw their parents, and their parents and their parents, on and on, backwards through time, all waiting to receive this blessing: forgiveness for being human, for being less than perfect, for giving us the wounds from which we have grown.

This year, on Mother's Day, my card to my own mother is going to say something different. I'm going to write it myself: "Dear Mom: Now that I am a mother, I can finally understand everything that you gave up in order to bring me into this world and prepare me for adulthood. Now I can recognize just how great your love for me has been. And now I can thank you, with my whole heart, for being the mother who is perfect for me."

When we are able to accept the circumstances of our lives, including the mothers we have been given, as being perfect in their own way, we are released from the stranglehold of resentment, free to focus our energy on other aspects of our life and growth. Eventually it becomes clear that this was all really meant to be just as it has been—and we might even find ourselves feeling grateful for all of it: the rough and the calm, the bitter and the sweet, the broken and the whole—all of the poignant contradictions of the life engendered for us by our mothers.

8
MOTHER AND CHILD

As mothers we are called to
give and to sacrifice,
but not to distort or stifle or belittle our lives for our
    children,
For Spirit uncannily weaves our journeys together so
    that the very act of becoming
our most authentic spiritual self
is precisely the act that most enhances
the growth of our children.
We will hurt our children
and we will be hurt by our children, make no mistake
    about that. But these are the wounds
upon which a spiritual being thrives.

9
FATHERS: GOOD AND BAD

I recently read an article published by the Virginia Department of Health, reviewing the impact of fathers on their children's health. The author had compiled several studies, which showed that children with nurturing fathers have less physical and emotional illness, higher IQ's, and less stress in their lives. In fact, the presence of a loving father has been shown to decrease the incidence of all of the following: suicide, poverty, substance abuse, violence, incarceration, sexual abuse and mental illness. One study showed simply that the more an infant was held by his or her father, the healthier that individual was in childhood and beyond.

These statistics are probably not surprising to most of us. Those who have had a loving, close relationship with their fathers know how valuable it has been. And those who have not experienced this type of caring know the ache of an empty place in their lives. But, after reading the article, I had the feeling that a new definition of the "good" father has been created: the one who nurtures his children, and that all other fathers, by default, fall under the heading "bad," as if, there is really only one "right" way to be a father.

But, nurturing children is a task that has already been ingrained in those of us who are mothers, as we have been provided with a maternal instinct that forges a deep bond with the offspring of our womb. Fathers, left out of the close physical connection that develops between mother and baby, must grow to love their children from a distance, from outside that bond. Lacking an internal drive for it, nurturing is an act that does not come easily or naturally to most men.

In addition, most fathers play other important roles for their children such as that of protector and provider. While a mother creates the stable nourishing nest within which a child grows, it is generally the father who urges exploration outside that nest. It is most likely to be the father, or the parent with the masculine drive to explore and conquer, who encourages the first climbing of a tree and who lets go of the bicycle seat the first time, while the maternal parent stands ready to bandage the scrapes and cuts that come along with these adventures.

Of course, this masculine energy and drive to master the unknown can have a dark-side, as well. Some fathers, too wounded themselves to fulfill their parental role in a healthy way, have resorted to violence, neglect or abandonment toward their own vulnerable offspring, who simply want to know that they are loved. The wounds created by this sort of upbringing are powerful and deep, marking their recipients for all time. But, as we have already learned, our wounds are the catalysts for our growth and require our acceptance.

As Geneen Roth has written, "It's not the wound that shapes our lives, it's the choice we make as adults between embracing our wounds or raging against them."

As I thought about this new definition of the good father, I began to wonder how it would apply to my own father. Having been frequently disciplined as a child with a leather strap in Grandpa's woodshed, Dad swore that he could do a better job as a parent. He vowed never to touch his children in anger. And he kept that vow. In fact, he rarely ever touched me at all. It took me many years, starving for his affection and approval, to realize that his distance from me was the highest form of love he was capable of displaying. To have overcome his childhood legacy of cruelty and harshness, to have absorbed a lifetime of abuse and refused to pass it on, was a feat of remarkable love and sacrifice. Though he could not hold me physically, he held me in his heart, with respect and devotion. So, his fathering fell short of the "good father" profile, because he was not able to be a nurturing man. But my emotional and physical health undoubtedly benefited from Dad's own way of showing love to me.

I have chosen to embrace my father wholeheartedly: all of his virtues and his shortcomings, as well as the choices he made for his own life. As a result, I have also welcomed the wounds that have necessarily become part of my history, using them to foster and intensify my own growth as a person. To move forward as a society, while we challenge men to fulfill a more nurturing parental role in the future, we still must accept the fathers of our past and all they have brought to our lives:

- those fathers who have coached countless soccer and baseball teams, and those who watched their favorite teams on television;
- those fathers who made it home on time to sit at the dinner table every night, and those who worked an extra job at night to put food on the dinner table;
- those fathers who held their tiny babies lovingly in their arms, and those who could only hold precious memories in their hearts;
- those fathers who laughed and played outdoors with their children, and those who shed a tear while watching their children through the window;

- those fathers who read bedtime stories every night, and those who laid awake with worries every night;
- those fathers who took care to say "I love you" each day, and those who read the newspaper silently in the living room;
- those fathers who protected their children by keeping danger at a distance and those who protected their children by keeping themselves at a distance;
- those fathers who chose, for the good of everyone, to stay, and those who chose, for the good of everyone, to leave.

It seems that it serves no purpose now to label as "good" or "bad", right or wrong. For, they all must find a place within our history as the fathers we were given in this lifetime. May we simply recognize that our fathers, gathering all their own experiences, wounds, and knowledge, facing life's demands and necessities, have done the best job they could. May our hearts hold their memories with respect and devotion, letting go of all the disappointments, bitterness and pain.

For, in order to continue our own progress in this journey of life and death, we must find a way to be grateful for those relationships and all that they have inflicted or infused upon our lives. When we reach the point where we no longer see ourselves as victims of the parents who raised us, we will be free to move ahead and consider other, even deeper, questions about the meaning of our life and existence. This, after all, is really what we came here to do.

10

IF YOU REALLY LOVED ME ...

If you really loved me:
you would watch me fall and not rush too quickly to
 scoop me up;
you would look upon my wounds without hiding them
 beneath bandages;
you would hear me cry and not try to quiet me with
 your softly voiced "hush";
you would see me struggling and not throw out lifelines
 to pull me to your shore;
you would know I'm lost and not shine your light to
 guide me toward your path.

If you really loved me:
you would gaze upon my stumbling and bleeding and
 sobbing and drowning and wandering without
 trying to rescue me from my own life.
You would simply behold me with eyes purely reflective
 of my strength and my knowing and my perfection.
You would sit in silent presence and create a space large
 enough to hold all my pain.

You would recognize, even when I am still unable to
see, that I am going to be all right.
If you really loved me ...

PART IV

DISCOVER MEANING

11

DISCOVER MEANING

"The reality is that you will grieve forever. You will not 'get over' the loss of a loved one; you will learn to live with it. You will heal and you will rebuild yourself around the loss you have suffered. You will be whole again but you will never be the same. Nor should you be the same nor would you want to."

— Elisabeth Kübler-Ross

Whether you know it or not, every event of your life has a purpose and meaning unique to your existence. Traumatic occurrences are often laden most heavily with symbolism and significance. When you are ready take time to look for the meaning within every encounter and circumstance. You may discover that they are signposts leading you toward the peace and healing you seek.

FOR YEARS after my father's death I longed to find meaning in what seemed to be a senseless event. But I couldn't talk to anyone about what had happened because the stigma surrounding suicide was so great. I continued to write in my journal and at my writing classes but I specifically avoided addressing suicide and my grief.

Occasionally I would be inspired to write a story or poem about an event from my daily life, which seemingly had nothing to do with grief and loss. But later I would look back on these stories and see my own pain emerging from the words, and a certain wisdom hidden inside the paragraphs. As I wrote about a patient searching for meaning in her illness I was creating a roadmap for myself that would one day lead me to the deeper understanding I craved. The answers were there all along, waiting until I was ready to perceive them.

Writing about any subject can open the subconscious and allow hidden meaning to be revealed. The key is to let the words to come through without trying to create any particular meaning from them. In your grief you may be seeking answers but remember the advice of Ranier Maria Rilke to "Live the questions now." The answers will appear in their own time someday in the distance.

> "Be patient toward all that is unsolved in your heart and try to love the questions themselves ... Do not now seek the answers, which cannot be given you because you would not be able to live them. And the point is, to live everything. Live the questions now. Perhaps you will then gradually, without noticing it, live along some distant day into the answer."
>
> — RAINER MARIA RILKE

Writing Prompts

1. What feels unfair to you in your life? What does fairness actually mean?
2. Have you found any meaning in past difficulties of your life?
3. What questions are you living now that cannot yet be answered?

12

WHY ME?

It's a common question: "Why me?", a frequently heard lament in this age of instant gratification and quick fixes. Accustomed to the workings of a market economy where solutions to problems are a commodity to be bought and sold, our society has little tolerance for the events of life that have no answers and no easy explanations. In my medical practice I hear this question nearly every week, ranging from "Why me? Why do I have to have a cold right now?" to "Why me? Why am I dying of cancer?"

A few years ago I heard this same question from an 86-year-old woman who had been admitted to a nursing home where I worked as Medical Director. Alice was a retired nurse who had previously been healthy and living independently in her own home. She had been sent to our facility after undergoing emergency surgery for a ruptured colon. Her condition was so serious that she had been in intensive care for several days after the surgery, suffering from septic shock. Alice was very angry that she had been sent to a nursing home to recover. She missed her home and her independence and was despondent over her decline in health.

She refused physical therapy and most of her medications, crying out "Why me? Why did this happen to me?" whenever anyone entered her room.

Alice had rapidly become an unpopular patient, ventilating her frustration on staff and residents alike. Her misery was almost palpable and seemed to spread a cloud of gloom throughout the entire facility.

Out of desperation, the nursing staff asked me to evaluate Alice to determine if there was a medication that might help improve her mood and her behavior. Before I confronted her, knowing I was in for a difficult visit, I spent some time reviewing her hospital chart. And I found some useful information. I learned that Alice had been in a coma while in the intensive care unit, severely ill with both kidney and liver failure. In fact, on three separate occasions her doctors felt she would not survive more than a few hours and had called her family to her bedside to say goodbye. However, after the third crisis, Alice had surprised everyone by emerging from her coma fully awake and with kidney and liver function restored to normal.

Empowered with this new information, I marched down the hall to face Alice. I had decided to turn the tables on her and confront her before she could begin her usual whining.

As soon as I sat down next to her bed I asked, "Alice ... why you?"

"What?" she snarled at me.

"Why you? You know, you nearly died three times while you were in the hospital. The doctors had given up on you, but you survived! You lived through septic shock, which is fatal to half of the people who experience it, even patients much younger than you. That you are alive and here today is a miracle, Alice! So, I'm asking you: Why you? Why are you here, in this place, at this time? Why were you granted this miracle?"

Alice stared at me in silence for a moment, then turned her

head to the wall. "I don't know what you're talking about," she whispered.

When she refused to answer any other questions or even look at me, I left her room disheartened, fearing I had pushed her too far. I would have to wait until my next visit to the nursing home, two weeks later, to finish my interview with her.

However, when I arrived for that next visit, one of the nurses stopped to ask me: "What did you do to Alice? She's ... different."

Alarmed, I hurried down the hall toward Alice's room before the nurse could even finish her report. But Alice was nowhere to be found—her bed was empty and the comforter was neatly in place. What had happened? I could think of only the worst possible outcomes.

Then, I heard a cheery "Hello" from the other end of the corridor and looked up to see Alice clumping along with her walker. She was smiling as she called out to me, "I know the answer to your question, Doctor."

When I reached her side she whispered in my ear, "I'm here to help these people." Gesturing toward the other residents, sitting in wheelchairs or recliners in the activity room, she went on: "They need me. That's why this happened to me. That's why I'm here." The look of joy on her face was radiant. I couldn't believe she was the same person I had seen two weeks earlier.

Later, Alice told me how this transformation had taken place. She had thought a great deal about my question to her, but could find no answer. It made no sense to her. Why had this happened? Could there be a reason for her to be in that nursing home? Had a miracle taken place when she survived? But she was still unable to see any explanation for her situation.

And then, one night she couldn't sleep because her roommate, a woman with Alzheimer's disease, was crying incessantly. While Alice's former response would have been to scream for a nurse and demand that the woman be moved to another room, this time Alice turned to look at her. She felt her heart opening with compassion as she realized that the other woman was frightened. Unable to get out of bed to comfort her, Alice created another solution. She began softly singing lullabies and nursery songs she could remember from her own childhood. As Alice continued this sweet serenade, she felt her own anger and pain gradually dissipating while the woman in the bed next to her drifted off to sleep.

The next morning, Alice awoke with a smile on her face and a feeling of peace in her heart. Alice had, indeed, found a purpose for her new life in the nursing home. She recognized for the first time the suffering of other patients in the facility, many of whom were lonely and confused. And, as a former nurse, she realized that she had something to offer them: her support and compassion. Alice began making herself available to new patients and their families, helping them adjust to the nursing home, consoling their fears and comforting their pain. She also regularly made rounds to those patients who rarely received visitors, bringing her friendly smile and warm heart to brighten their days.

She became a joy to be near, always positive and cheerful, a total contrast from her previous self.

The turning point had come when Alice asked the question "Why me?" from a new perspective, with curiosity and acceptance rather than anger and resistance. As a result, Alice had discovered a miracle within her tragedy—and changed the rest of her life. She would live out her days in the nursing home in joy and peace rather than misery and bitterness.

I have learned from many patients like Alice that somewhere, hidden within each misfortune of life, lies a true treasure. Asking with an open heart "Why me? ... Why here? ... Why now?" can unlock the door to understanding the suffering we encounter in our lives. Many times, we will discover that our particular adversities are really perfect opportunities to grow and achieve a new level of spiritual awareness.

So, the next time you face an unexpected downturn on the road of life, go ahead and ask, "Why me?" It's a perfectly good question, as long as you are ready to hear the answer.

TO WHAT PURPOSE HAVE I BEEN BROUGHT

To What Purpose Have I Been Brought?

There were so many days and nights when I wondered why… when I couldn't see a purpose for me to be where I found myself.
These were the days and nights of endless studying, reading, and memorizing;
of stuffing my head with facts and formulas and pharmacologies;
of denying my body sleep and food and sex and comfort;
of depriving my soul of music and literature and art and culture;
of starving my spirit for kindness and nurturing and recognition;
of suffering by choice and by ignorance in service of (supposedly) healing.

To what purpose have I been brought?

There was the night I went home after sixteen hours in
    the emergency room
without food or rest or a single moment for
    contemplation;
the night I went home thinking only of taking my shoes
    off and falling into bed;
the night I took my shoes off to find them soaked with
    the blood of a 16-year-old girl
who had died from her injuries while we highly-trained
    healers fought helplessly
to save her.

To what purpose have I been brought?

There was the day I cried in the stairwell when I
    couldn't bear to carry
the life of one more person in my hands;
the day I cried in the stairwell because the sick ones just
    kept coming and
the pager kept calling;
the day I cried because I couldn't remember the last
    time I had seen the sunset.

To what purpose have I been brought?

And then there was the day when the voice on the
    telephone spoke the words that changed everything;
when the voice spoke the words that blood had been
    spilled, not of a stranger or a patient,
but, the blood of my father, my most cherished father,
who took his life out of my hands forever.

To what purpose have I been brought?

You can't just <u>ask</u> that question.
You have to cry it and bleed it and soak it up and wring
 it out and cry again
and you have to show up every day… every day…
 every day…
whether you know the answer or not.

To what purpose have I been brought?

And somewhere in the blood and the tears you begin to
 notice something-
something very small-
almost undetectable;
like a hollyhock blooming on a fence in the alley;
like a woman bringing flowers to say thank you a year
 later;
like the young mother who says I never knew what love
 was before;
like the dead man whose face had been eaten away by
 cancer
visiting in a dream to say, "You cared for me
like God."

To what purpose have I been brought?

I know….
it is…
to save my own Soul.

14

LESSONS FROM PEELING APPLES

Several years ago I attended a weeklong writing retreat during which we were asked to observe 24 hours of silence. It happened that I drew kitchen duty on the day of silence and when I reported for my shift that morning I found that the cook had left written instructions for us since we weren't allowed to speak. She pointed me to a huge bowl of bright red and green apples bearing the following note:

"These apples need to be peeled."

As I peeled each and every apple that morning I focused all my attention on the task, noting the smooth feel of the skin, the delightful aroma that emerged when it was pierced and the texture of the apple flesh underneath. It happened that my intention for that retreat was to find my purpose and figure out how to live it fully. Peeling apples and going through the day in silence gave me the perfect opportunity to contemplate that intention. Later during my meditation I remembered the message I received in the morning and wrote the following piece:

Apples

On the morning of our day of silence, I awoke to find that the angel Maria had left a note attached to a large, black bowl half-filled with an assortment of apples.

A note with a profound message:

"These apples need to be peeled."

These apples <u>need</u> to be peeled.

These apples <u>need</u> … to … be…peeled.

These apples…
in order to become what they have been chosen for,
in order to achieve the purpose for which they have been brought,

… these apples need to be peeled.

Some apples give up their peels less willingly than others.
Some must lose flesh, as well.
And some release their peels so easily,
it is as if they have been waiting for the knife all along.

WHAT I BEGAN to recognize that day while peeling apples is that life gradually shapes us into our purpose through the challenges and suffering it presents to us over time. And we can resist our losses or surrender to them—the choice is ours in every moment. But the path toward manifesting the ultimate meaning of life must contain some struggles, for we are meant to be honed and fired—just as surely as the apple needs to be peeled—to release all the sweetness and succulence that life contains.

15
GRIEF AND THE GARDEN

This summer my flower gardens have been a favorite stopping place for some deer who live in the woods near my home. One day I walked outside to see a doe standing in the middle of my "Forgiveness Garden" (how ironic!) ready to chomp down on some tasty blossoms and a few days later I found her lying down for a nap in my little bed of annuals. Some of my petunias had been pulled up by the roots and the tops had been bitten off most of the pansies.

I admit I've felt some frustration and disappointment over losing the flowers I worked so hard to plant and nurture all summer. But I do understand the ways of life and nature and that everything is ultimately lost. So I have worked on letting go and being grateful for the chance to practice forgiveness.

Then last weekend I stopped by a local nursery to pick up a few flowers to fill in the bare spots for the remainder of this growing season. As I chatted with the owner, she told me that a man had just come into her shop looking for flowers to plant. His wife had recently died after being sick all summer and unable to plant her flower garden so he had decided to do it for her, in her memory.

I recalled some of my hospice patients for whom gardening had played a special role: Danny, a young man with AIDS who planted a flower garden for his mother before he died, and another woman who created a perennial garden in her backyard before she died that would bloom with color all year long as a lasting gift for her family. Gardens are surely tied to our grief, representing both our hope for new life and our willingness to let life go in its own time.

As I was leaving the nursery the shopowner handed me two packs of scraggly and wilted pansies that she had been about to throw away, suggesting that maybe I could find a place for them in my garden. Back in my yard, knees to the ground, I dug holes for the poor struggling pansies and thought of the sorrowful husband who was planting flowers of grief in his wife's garden. I sent him my love and compassion as I patted the soil around the roots of each tiny plant. This is how we grow and survive our losses—by pouring our love and energy into the wilted and scraggly parts of life that remain for us, nurturing them in the hope that they will one day blossom with beauty.

To all who are grieving now, especially those who have experienced traumatic death, I send out this prayer adapted from the Ho'oponopono tradition:

__I am sorry__ for the brokenness of this world we live in that has caused such unbearable destruction and pain.

__Please forgive me__ for any part I have unknowingly played in the negativity of this world.

__I love you__ with the highest form of healing love that is possible; may it soothe your grieving hearts.

__Thank you__ for sharing this pain with me and allowing me an opportunity to heal my own broken heart.

PART V

RECOGNIZE THE DIVINE

16

RECOGNIZE THE DIVINE

"When you are sorrowful look again in your heart, and you shall see that in truth you are weeping for that which has been your delight."

— KAHLIL GIBRAN

Once you are aware that there is hidden meaning within every story, you may also begin to recognize the presence of the Divine that totally surrounds you. While the Divine has permeated everything and every person all along, you now become capable of perceiving it as you are given a new form of sight.

~

OVER THE MANY years of my grief journey I continued to work as a doctor while still carrying my pain with me at all times. Initially my guilt over dad's death caused me to question whether or not I could still find a place in medicine where I could function. I felt broken inside but I also experienced deeper compassion for my patients than ever before. Somehow I came to see that I still had something to offer to patients and also that they were bringing me opportunities to learn new lessons and to gradually heal myself.

At times it was perfect. When I could let Divine love flow through my broken heart it seemed to help people, like Kaye in the first story. I was learning the mystery of true healing and the importance of not attaching to the outcome. "Let go and let flow" was my new mantra and this applied to writing, as well.

Though I still wasn't ready to write openly about my dad's suicide I was seeing and feeling pain with my patients. This would prepare me for the day when I would be brave enough to finally tell the story that needed to be told.

It's essential to realize that our truth reveals itself through story in layers. Sometimes the deepest pain can take years to come to the surface. But all the stories that come before it are pieces of the puzzle. Be patient as you write your own stories that must be told and recognize the Divine in every word.

Writing Prompts

1. Where can you see Divine love in the world around you?
2. What layers of your grief have you already worked through?
3. What grief and pain have you recognized in other people?

17

WHAT YOU SEE IS WHAT YOU GET

Many years ago, when I was first starting in medical practice as a brand new doctor, I had a very difficult patient come to me. Kaye had been given five different psychiatric diagnoses by five different psychiatrists, so no one could really decide what was wrong with her, whether she was schizophrenic, bipolar, antisocial, borderline, addictive or all of the above.

Her appearance was very bizarre— she wore several different shirts at the same time, one on top of the other, with variously colored collars visible around her neck; and her hair was cut quite short, but in many different lengths as if she had taken the scissors to it herself without looking in a mirror. She usually carried several large shopping bags, full of an odd assortment of things she had found on the street or in trashcans. And she had been in and out of psychiatric hospitals and jail for much of her life.

Most disturbing, though, was Kaye's behavior. She was a very angry and hostile person, frequently causing some sort of commotion in the waiting room. She showed up once or twice a week without an appointment, demanding to be seen for whatever crisis she was having that day, and generally creating chaos around her wherever she went. Because I couldn't figure out which diagnosis to apply to her, my assessment in her chart read: "Severely damaged." She was simply a person who had been so injured by the misfortunes of her life that she couldn't function well in the world.

I learned that Kaye had been kicked out of nearly every other medical practice in town. I was just the next doctor on her list. In fact, because my last name starts with a "W", I was actually the last name on her list as she went through the Yellow Pages seeking one physician after another. Sadly, I was almost at the point of firing her as a patient myself—I just didn't like her and I couldn't find a way to get comfortable taking care of her.

However, one day, I was attending a medical lecture at the Catholic Hospital, which was on the other side of town from the hospital where I practiced. I had only been in that hospital a few times before and had always entered through the back entrance near the staff parking lot. But on that particular day, the back lot was full and I had to park in front of the hospital. This is an important detail, because it meant that for the first time, I entered through the hospital's front door and lobby area. As I walked in, the first thing I saw was a huge tapestry mural that covered an entire wall. It was beautiful: with vivid colors and a striking contemporary design. And I'll never forget the words that were woven across it:

"Care must be taken of the sick as if they were Christ himself."

I was awestruck by that statement. I stood staring at the message: "Care must be taken of the sick as if they were Christ himself." I knew immediately which person this refrain was referring to in my life. In fact, the saying reminded me of a quote from Mother Teresa that I had recently discovered where she referred to the severely ill and poverty-stricken patients she treated as "Christ in distressing disguise."

From that moment on, I could not escape from this idea: Kaye was really Christ disguised as a very mentally ill and annoying woman. I was not accustomed to thinking in this way, but I also could not shake this new thought. And, gradually, my attitude and behavior toward Kaye also began to change. Instead of dreading her visits, I found myself feeling just a little intrigued and almost eager each time I saw her name on the schedule. I was never sure what to expect from her, but, amazingly, Kaye's behavior started to change as well. Her tone of voice softened and she actually began to smile on occasion. She became polite toward my office staff and started coming to the office only when she had a scheduled appointment. Eventually, I truly came to enjoy her visits and found her to be thoughtful and sensitive in her own way. She even brought in poetry for me to read that she had composed over the years, mostly very heart-rending verses about her loneliness and isolation.

Over the course of several years I came to feel as close to Kaye as any other patient I treated. But then, I left my practice for a few years in order to stay home with my young children and Kaye moved to another town. I lost touch with her for about five years, until one day, while I was volunteering at a clinic in a homeless shelter, I walked out to the waiting room to see Kaye smiling at me. She had read my name in a newspaper article about the clinic and tracked me down. I learned that she was living in her own little apartment and managing to care for herself. She hadn't been admitted to a psychiatric facility even once during those years, and had avoided all legal trouble. She came that day just to tell me thank you.

She said, "You treated me like I was worth something. And you helped me see myself as worthwhile for the first time in my life."

In that moment, I remembered that mural on the wall of

the hospital and I realized exactly how important the message portrayed there really is:

"Care must be taken of the sick as if they were Christ himself."

And I realized as well, this truth: What you SEE is what you get. When I could see only Kaye's outward anger and dysfunctional behavior, that is exactly what I got from her. I had to have the blinders removed from my eyes in order to truly see Kaye – to see through the layers of pain and fear that had encrusted her and to see the simple beauty of her divine soul. Somehow, seeing that mural on the wall that day shattered my own layers of pain and fear that had obscured my vision, finally allowing me to see beyond the external. And, once I could SEE the beauty within Kaye, then I could receive the gentleness, the fragile hopefulness, the poetry that she was capable of exhibiting.

As a physician, I can think of no more profound lesson than the one I learned that day in the hospital lobby:

"Care must be taken of the sick as if they were Christ himself."

Once I began to operate from that vision, I quickly recognized that my whole practice was full of patients who closely resembled Christ—they were everywhere. Some of them had more challenging and distressing disguises than others, but I became practiced at seeing through them all. And the more I could SEE the divine in my patients, the more I got, the more I was blessed by caring for them.

And I wonder now, what would happen if our lawmakers were to adopt this axiom as a vision statement for our country's health care reform: "Care must be taken of the sick as if they were Christ himself." If this belief were the highest guiding principle for healthcare in our country, I think Congress would find a way to institute a universal health care program as quickly as possible. They could not go on another moment knowing that there are sick and mentally ill and severely damaged people in our society who cannot get the services they need. They would not tolerate such a deplorable situation.

Because, "What you see, is what you get." If we see the poor and downtrodden of our society as undeserving of health care, as not having earned the right to be given medications when they are ill, to receive emotional support when they are needy, to have their bodies restored when they are injured; then, what we will get is a nation where the most vulnerable members of our society suffer and decline even further, surely diminishing us all as a people.

"Care must be taken of the sick as if they were Christ himself."

This vision became the driving force behind my work in medicine for all the rest of my career. From caring for community members living at the bottom of the socio-economic ladder in a homeless shelter, to those who reside in nursing homes, to the terminally ill who are enrolled in hospice care, I have held as my particular mission that patients not only receive care for their medical needs, but that each and every one feels VALUED as a person. Because, as Kaye taught me, that is how a life can be transformed.

By treating the whole person and responding to the full spectrum of need for each individual, we can help all people see their own worth and feel like valuable members of society. If I am correct, and what you see really is what you get, then I hope I can help everyone see some new ideas and some new possibilities for this world—and perhaps, to see the divine in some of its disguises. Just look around you— its everywhere.

And then, just maybe, you or I will look in the mirror one day, and see as well, the divinity that resides within each of us, the Beauty that we have been seeking all along.

18

FINDING MARIA

Once during a lecture I was giving on the spiritual care of hospice and palliative patients, an audience member asked me how I would suggest providing for the spiritual needs of a patient with end-stage dementia, such as Alzheimer's disease. His question was quite relevant since Alzheimer's disease causes severe impairment in the functioning of the brain and results in loss of memory, changes in mood and personality and ultimately, an inability to communicate and perform the basic activities of daily living. It seems unlikely that such a patient could participate in or benefit from what we typically think of as "spiritual care."

As I considered this question, a story came to my mind of a patient I once cared for named Maria:

WHEN I WAS FIRST ASSIGNED to make rounds on Maria, a nursing home patient who was bedbound and unable to move or speak due to endstage Alzheimer's disease, I dreaded having to see her. My favorite part of interacting with patients was being able to connect with them and listen to their stories and I assumed it would be impossible to form any kind of meaningful relationship with someone in the final stages of Alzheimer's.

I found Maria in her hospital bed in the nursing home, lying on her right side and curled up into fetal position. Her eyes were closed and she did not respond to my voice or to my touch when I examined her. I knew from the nursing report that this was her usual condition – she was breathing on her own and she would take in food and water when it was offered to her, but that was the full extent of her functioning.

I finished my exam in just a few minutes, since I couldn't ask her any questions or converse with her. But I knew that the shortest length of visit I could bill for was 15 minutes. It would feel dishonest to me to bill for that amount of time and not really spend it with the patient, so I decided to sit with Maria in her room for the entire 15 minutes. Besides, I reasoned, Maria deserved to have that time and attention just as much as any other patient.

Thus began my visits with Maria – after examining her I would sit in a chair next to the bed, read her chart and write my note, watching the minutes tick away. But one day while I was listening to Maria's heart with my stethoscope, an orderly dropped a tray in the hallway outside her door. With the loud crash, Maria startled and I heard her heart rate increase while her breathing became more rapid and her eyes opened wide in fear. I quickly grabbed her hands and leaned over to talk to her, saying, "It's okay, Maria. You're safe. Nothing is going to hurt you." As she gradually relaxed and the look of terror left her face, I realized that some part of Maria <u>was</u> capable of responding to my voice.

From then on I began talking to Maria every time I saw her, reading her chart aloud to her, commenting on the food she had eaten that day and telling her when the nurse noted that her son, who lived in another state, had called to ask about her. I began to look forward to these unusual visits, because I found it very peaceful to be in Maria's presence. During those fifteen minutes I could simply sit and be with her, without expectations or pressure.

One day I noticed a family photograph on Maria's dresser and picked it up to look more closely at the people in the image. In the center I recognized a much younger and healthier Maria, wearing a beautiful blue dress. She was seated next to a handsome gentleman, who must have been her husband, and surrounded by younger adults and children of all ages. She was holding a baby girl on her lap, wearing a white christening gown.

Excited by this new finding I began describing the picture to Maria, including her blue dress, the newly-christened baby and the man I thought might be her son Carlos, who called the nursing home every week to check on her. As I reached to place the photograph back on the dresser, I glanced over at Maria to see tears trickling down her face. Instantly I bent down to embrace her frail body, as I knew for certain that I had found Maria – from inside the tangled cells and synapses of her brain I had made a real connection with her soul.

I saw Maria only a few more times before she died. On those last visits I was able to speak much more directly to her and let her know that she was loved, that I understood how difficult this part of her life must be, that she was free to go whenever the time was right for her. When I returned to that nursing home after her death, I felt the pain of loss as I passed by her empty room. I would miss Maria because I knew her – I had found her there and she, in a way, had found me too.

Maria fulfilled a profound purpose in those last few months of her life – she taught me that the soul cannot be diminished by any illness or injury that damages the physical body. She taught me to respect the dignity and wholeness of every life, regardless of the level of functioning of the mind and brain.

She taught me to be steadfast in my search to connect with the soul of every single patient I cared for and to be courageous in teaching others to do so, as well.

AND SO MY answer for how to provide spiritual care to patients with dementia is simple: Recognize and believe that every patient has an intact soul, be willing to give your time and presence to that person, and be authentic in your expression of lovingkindness and concern. We are all connected on one level or another and no matter how tangled or difficult the communication might be, it is possible, with patience and determination, to "find Maria," wherever we encounter her.

KATYA'S TREES
A FABLE ABOUT LIFE AND DEATH

Once upon a time, in a forest far away, lived a young woman named Katya. She had been raised in a small cabin surrounded by a forest, and while she knew everything about the trees she loved, she knew very little about the rest of the world.

Katya, from a very young age, had always had a special relationship with the trees that grew near her home. She visited them every day, regardless of the weather, and was able to relate to the trees as living beings, as if they were her brothers and sisters. She would listen to the rustling of branches, the creaking of trunks, the wind moving through the treetops, and she knew which trees were healthy and which were injured or nearing death.

Each morning, on her walk through her woods, she brought with her tiny gifts for the trees: small wreaths of juniper berries and pine branches, strings of pine cones, tiny weavings of long pine needles and dried grasses and flowers. As she studied each tree, she decided if a gift was needed and then would hang one of her creations from a branch or tuck it into a notch near the trunk.

Each afternoon, before returning to her cabin, she would gather up the berries and needles and cones that had fallen that day, along with occasional blades of grass and wildflowers. These were the supplies from which she would make the next day's gifts for the trees.

Katya had developed certain ceremonies for the trees as well: when the seasons changed, when a tree became ill, when a bird made a new nest in a tree's branches, when a tiny seedling first emerged from the earth and began to grow, and whenever a tree began to die. These were the special moments in the life cycle of a tree, and Katya honored each of these passages with her gifts and celebrations.

This was Katya's way of being with trees, and their way of being with her.

~

ONE DAY A SCIENTIST was sent out to study trees in various forests around the world. It seemed that many trees were dying and the cause was unknown. Scientists were very alarmed, for life on our planet could not exist without the presence of trees.

This particular scientist was sent to live amongst the trees, to study everything about them in an attempt to save them. He made his way through one forest after another, taking careful notes and measurements, spending many hours observing dead and dying trees and examining the living trees as well.

"What is the answer," he wondered? "Why are these trees dying?"

Eventually he came upon a forest he had never seen before. At first glance the trees there seemed far healthier than those he had been examining for months. He wandered through these woods, amazed at the supple limbs and the green boughs, the young and the old trees, alike, thriving in this region.

From time to time, he noticed tiny wreaths and weavings

that had been carefully placed on certain trees and wondered where they might have come from. Then he heard a lovely melody arising from a nearby meadow.

There he found a young woman standing in the center of the green meadow, turning a slow circle while she sang, reaching a hand out toward the trees encircling her. When she saw the scientist, she stopped her song, puzzled by this stranger in her woods.

He told her his name was Jonathan and explained that he was there to study the trees.

"I am Katya and I also study the trees," she replied.

Jonathan wanted to know right away if Katya knew why the trees in this forest seemed so healthy. But she knew nothing of any other forests and could not understand that her trees might be different or unusual in any way. He wanted to know if she "did" anything to the trees.

Katya responded, "I care for them."

He asked what happened when trees became sick.

She answered, "Some of them get better, some of them stay the same, and some of them get worse."

Then he asked her about the small items that he had seen hanging from some of the trees. She was reluctant to share her rituals with a stranger because they were just her own simple way of being with the trees. But eventually she told him that she gathered all the fallen treasures in the forest each evening and made gifts of them to give back to the trees the next day.

Katya's stories did not seem like reasonable explanations for the health of this forest to Jonathan's scientific mind. Frustrated that he could find no answers, he returned to his studies. He took many measurements and samples and recordings from the trees, which alarmed Katya, for she recognized that the trees were being hurt by some of the scientist's probings. At last, his work was finished and Jonathan moved on. Katya was relieved and returned to her usual routine, helping the trees recover from the explorations of the scientist.

∽

In time, Jonathan returned to his university and wrote a paper about the healthy forest he had visited. He created several theories about why it was so healthy. His colleagues were eager to see his work, for they were very concerned about the loss of trees in other forests. They hoped to learn how they might prevent the trees in every forest from dying.

In the end, however, Jonathan could still draw no conclusions from the healthy forest – it was a mystery to him and the data he had gathered offered no explanation. At that point all of his travels and studies and calculations seemed a failure. He was supposed to present his findings at a huge conference in front of scientists from all around the world, but he had nothing to report. He feared he would be disgraced in front of his peers and was desperate to have some answer to give them.

At the last moment, before his turn to speak, as he was rummaging through a box of specimens he had collected, he came across a small wreath of juniper berries, which he had taken from Katya's forest. Clutching the wreath in his hand, Jonathan gave his report, describing the health of the trees in this particular forest. In his conclusion, he offered the theory that, though he could not yet explain the mechanism, the juniper berry wreaths were somehow responsible for the vibrancy of this forest.

The room erupted with noise as all the scientists in the audience began discussing this amazing finding amongst themselves. Some of the scientists scoffed at the idea, others cheered, but all were intrigued. The university research board immediately voted to fund more studies of the amazing juniper wreath.

Jonathan was appointed head of the research team and spent many years applying the juniper berry wreath to trees of many different varieties and at many stages of health and disease. Ultimately, he found that some trees got better, some stayed the same, and some trees got worse, no matter what he did.

Meanwhile, reporters from newspapers and television networks heard about the research that was being done with the juniper berry wreath. They reported this information to people around the world. Some thoughtful people who cared a great deal about trees decided that they would like to try using juniper berry wreaths to heal the sick trees in forests near them.

But when they began to ask shopkeepers where they could buy the wreaths, they found that there were none for sale. Very soon, however, a clever person, who also cared about trees, recognized that there was a demand for juniper berry wreaths. He started a business, a small factory, to make hundreds of juniper berry wreaths, trying to meet his customers' needs for more and more wreaths.

When these juniper berry wreaths from the factory were placed on sick trees around the world, some of the trees got better, some of them stayed the same, and some got worse. As people began to tell stories of their experience with the juniper berry wreaths, they talked mostly of the trees that got better, for these were the stories everyone wanted to hear.

Some of the listeners concluded that if juniper berry wreaths can heal trees, imagine what they can do for people. They began to hang the wreaths in their cars and their homes and some of them even wore the wreaths around their necks. The demand for the wreaths increased so much that soon the factory couldn't keep up. Also, some days there weren't enough juniper berries available to make the usual number of wreaths. But some clever people had already begun growing juniper orchards just to harvest berries for the wreath factory.

Now, the price of the wreaths had begun to increase, because the demand was high and the supply was short. Many people were unable to afford the wreaths and began to complain because they were being denied the healing power of juniper berry wreaths. So, before long, a new company was formed to make less expensive wreaths. This company had the bright idea to make them from plastic juniper berries, which cost much less to make than it cost to harvest real berries.

Now, almost anyone could afford some type of juniper berry wreath. Many people actually thought the plastic ones were superior for they didn't break or crumble as easily, and they came in many colors! When people who were sick wore the wreaths around their necks, whether real or plastic, some of them got better, some of them stayed the same, and some of them got worse.

One day, another scientist decided that if the juniper berry wreaths could help some people get better, there must be something in the berries that had a healing effect. So, she spent many hours in the laboratory, breaking down the juniper berry into its chemical components, trying to discover which one could heal disease. Eventually her research showed that juniper berry extract, when swallowed by her test subjects, helped some of them get better, while some of them stayed the same, and some got worse.

And so, a new company was created to make capsules of juniper berry extract that people could swallow every day to help them be healthy. Before long, nearly every person was taking the extract or wearing a wreath of some sort. And nearly every tree was adorned with a plastic juniper berry wreath. And still, some trees got better, some stayed the same, and some got worse.

∼

DURING THESE MANY YEARS, Jonathan had continued his research projects with trees. Even though he recognized the widespread acceptance of the juniper berry wreath, which he had been credited with discovering, he was not satisfied with the outcome of his research. He still felt that something was missing and he was frustrated that he had not found the true answer to his questions.

He had never been able to explain how the wreath had benefited the trees, nor why only some of the trees got better. Though he was highly acclaimed by the scientific world, he was never truly satisfied with his accomplishments. As he looked around him, he realized that just as many trees were dying as when he had started his work, and people also seemed to be dying at the same rate as before. What had he achieved?

Now an old man, Jonathan decided to journey back to that miraculous forest he had once beheld, to see if he could finally find the answer he had been seeking. After walking many miles through the forest he found Katya, still living in her cabin, now stooped and gray-haired.

Just as he had remembered, the forest around Katya's home was lush and vibrant. He stood in the midst of the grand trees, breathing in the scent of pine, grateful for the shade being given to him, and tears began to fall slowly from his eyes.

"Oh Katya," he asked, "what is the secret? Why could I never find it? What is the source of the great life I feel in this forest?"

Looking on with compassion, Katya replied, "Perhaps you were looking for the wrong thing

"But what is it that you do, Katya that makes this forest healthy? It has to be you. I don't believe it is the juniper berry wreath," Jonathan insisted.

" I told you many years ago: some trees get better, some trees stay the same and some trees get worse."

"What do you do when a tree is dying? How do you stop that from happening?" he asked.

"Oh, I would never try to interfere with the normal life cycle of a tree. Each tree must die in its own time. That is not for me to decide. I simply honor the process and celebrate the transitions. Forests need dead trees you know. They play an important role."

"Why could I never achieve the same success as you? I tried everything I could think of to nurture the forests, but none of them were like this."

"I simply give the trees my gifts. This is what I was born to do. No one can duplicate another's gift. You must find your own authentic gift and offer it to the life around you. When you do that, your world will flourish."

Katya bowed her head and turned to walk away. She had told Jonathan everything he needed to know.

∽

MANY MORE YEARS LATER, Jonathan was a very old man, confined to his bed and nearing death. His loving family surrounded him: his wife, three children and five grandchildren. One by one he called each grandchild to his bedside to offer a special message. To each child he spoke of the importance of discovering one's gift and of bringing it into the world in a special way. He told them that he would die soon and that it was the right time for him to go.

When he called his last granddaughter to his side, he told her a very special story – the story of Katya's trees. He also reminded her that her's was the gift of storytelling. He made her promise to write this story for him someday after he was gone.

"But Grandfather," she asked, "what is your special gift?"

"Ah, my child," he chuckled, "mine is the gift of observation. As a scientist, I have used this gift every day. I have learned that there is much mystery in the world, much that science will never explain. And, that is the way it should be."

∾

So, true to my promise to Grandpa Jon, I offer "Katya's Trees" to the world. I don't expect too much to come of it, but possibly some who read the story will get better because of it, while some will stay the same and some will just get worse.

AND THAT'S the way it should be.

PART VI

OPEN TO COMPASSION

20

OPEN TO COMPASSION

"Grief, I've learned, is really just love. It's all the love you want to give but cannot. All of that unspent love gathers up in the corners of your eyes, the lump in your throat, and in that hollow part of your chest. Grief is just love with no place to go."

— Jamie Anderson

As you master the lessons of finding meaning in everything that happens to you and seeing the Divinity that surrounds you, your heart will finally begin to open and allow the exchange of love with other people. You are capable of experiencing compassion at a deeper level than ever before, having been hollowed out inside by the suffering you have endured thus far.

∼

When you begin to view your grief as *love* you carry it differently and develop a new relationship with your pain. Now expressing grief is also a way of sharing love with others who are hurting. In my medical practice I found that my capacity to be present with people in pain had vastly increased and I was able to see them more clearly than ever. I learned that it wasn't my job to fix people but to help them find compassion for their own suffering.

In my family medicine clinic, during hospice visits, in the nursing home, I began to see evidence of love everywhere and to recognize that my grief allowed me to tap into that healing source. Now my writing was focused on remarkable experiences with other people, but my grief was becoming visible just under the surface. Soon I would be able to find the same compassion for myself that I shared with others.

Stay open to whatever feelings arise for you. Showing love to others takes courage because it makes you vulnerable to being hurt again. But at some point you will be ready for that step. Write your fear and pain, explore the obstacles to love that you feel, and allow your grief to slowly evolve.

Writing Prompts

1. How has grief hollowed you out inside?
2. Where do you see love in the world around you?
3. How can you love yourself better?

21

A MOTHER'S HEALING LOVE

Donna was a woman in her fifties with borderline mental retardation who had lived with her mother Mary all her life. Both women were my patients and came together to every appointment. Donna was shy and quiet with a very simple understanding of life, somewhat like the character "Forrest Gump" in the movie of the same name. She and Mary were very close and looked after one another in the tiny home they shared. Every Christmas Donna and Mary would bring a plate of homemade sugar cookies to the office for our staff, sharing the sweetness of their lives with others.

When Mary learned she was terminally ill and had only a short time to live, she worried about Donna's wellbeing, wondering if her daughter could survive on her own. But with the help of social services we were able to assure Mary that Donna would continue to receive disability payments and would be visited by a caseworker every month. The last time I saw Mary in the hospital she asked me to look after Donna's health and I gave my promise to remain her doctor.

Donna was despondent for a time after her mother's death, experiencing deep sadness and loneliness, but she managed to care for herself adequately. She kept her home clean, cooked simple meals for herself and did her laundry every week. When she came to the office for her regular appointments we talked frequently about heaven, for Donna believed that her mother was there, happy and free of pain.

About a year after Mary's death a lump was found in one of Donna's breasts that was shown by biopsy to be cancer. She was scheduled for surgery to remove the lump before she began radiation treatments. I spent a great deal of time talking with Donna, trying to explain cancer and the necessary surgery in simple terms. She seemed to have difficulty understanding the situation and kept repeating, "Why do I have a tumor?" I worried that Donna might be overwhelmed by the stress of this illness and the decisions that she would have to make in the future and feared that she would not have an easy course.

Donna was admitted to the hospital the night before her procedure and the surgeon visited to prepare her for what would happen in the operating room. He showed Donna the lump and marked her breast at the places where the incision would be made the next morning. Again Donna seemed to have little understanding of what was happening to her and the surgeon voiced the same concerns I was feeling, but he felt it was important for Donna's health to remove the lump as soon as possible to prevent it from spreading further. Though her understanding was limited, Donna remained calm and expressed no fear or discomfort about her situation.

The next day I received a call from the surgeon and expected him to report on the outcome of the surgery. However, to my great surprise he informed me that the surgery had been cancelled because he had been unable to find the lump once they got Donna into the operating room. The radiologist had repeated a mammogram and ultrasound and found no trace of cancerous tissue anywhere in either breast. The surgeon was baffled and asked me to check in on Donna before she was discharged later that morning.

When I told Donna that her tumor had disappeared she was stoic and unemotional, as usual, and not at all surprised. She said, "I know. Mother took the tumor away." I asked her how that had happened and she explained that her mother had visited her in the hospital room during the night, telling her not to worry because she was taking care of the cancer. Donna went on to say that her mother often visited her at night to check on her and see if she needed help.

Donna stared at me with her huge eyes, wondering why I seemed to be having difficulty understanding her story. She went home that day, back to her little house, where she continued to look after herself for many years, with the occasional help, I assume, of her mother and other angels. Donna never had a recurrence of breast cancer and remained healthy into her elder years.

22

BRIAN'S LAST RUN

In my years of practice as a Home Health and Hospice physician, I gathered many memories of visits with patients in their own homes, sitting beside their beds, sipping tea from their favorite china cups, hearing the stories held within the walls of their living spaces. One special memory comes to me now, which speaks to the advantages and opportunities afforded by home-based health care:

BRIAN WAS a man in his 60's who had recently been diagnosed with a very aggressive type of cancer. He was being cared for at home by his wife, along with the help of our staff, and had requested that he not be sent back to the hospital. I was asked to see him to help manage his pain, as his medication did not seem to be giving him adequate relief. Brian was refusing to take stronger doses of pain medication because he wanted to be fully alert and awake. His oldest daughter and her children were due to arrive from out-of-state in the next 24 hours. His greatest wish on the day I came to visit was to hang on long enough to see them and say goodbye.

As I entered his room, I could see that Brian was obviously suffering. His wife, who hadn't slept much for several days, was distraught and tearful, feeling helpless in the presence of such intense pain. I felt some desperation myself, wondering what I could offer to this man other than drugs. But, as I looked around his room, I noticed some of his prized possessions scattered about and decorating the walls. There was a photograph of Brian crossing the finish line in a foot race, medals hanging by colorful ribbons from a bulletin board, a pair of running shoes rather than slippers next to his bed. On closer inspection, I saw that the quilt which had been tucked around him was made from dozens of T-shirts representing various marathons around the country.

"You're a runner!" I gasped to Brian as I came to that realization.

"Yes," he smiled, "I've run over 30 marathons. That's hard to believe if you look at me now, eh?"

"I've run two marathons myself," I replied.

"Ah," he struggled to speak, "then you know how much I miss it. Running was my escape, but also my form of prayer. ... Do you understand what I mean?"

"Yes," I answered, for indeed, as a devout runner, I knew exactly what Brian was talking about.

Reaching for my hand, Brian whispered, "Take me for a run with you."

Fully understanding his request, I began to describe for him my daily run on a trail through the foothills near my home. I took him up a steep path, next to a stream which was raging high with Spring runoff. We stepped our way carefully over some large rocks in the path and ducked under a canopy of scrub oak, while inhaling the scent of wild roses growing in the underbrush. We came to a plateau and began to stride out as the trail flattened and widened before us. The early morning sun was shining down on us, quickly evaporating the dew that remained on the grasses next to the road. We descended from the plateau to meet up with our return path, heading home again.

I was lost in my description of the run, pointing out all my favorite places on the trail, and did not notice until I finished that Brian had fallen asleep with a faint smile on his lips. His wife was standing nearby, with tears streaming down her face. She and I hugged one another silently as I stood to leave. I knew I would never see her or Brian again. But, I also knew that he could make it until his daughter arrived; that he would have one last chance to see his grandchildren.

Had Brian been in a hospital room for the last moments of his life, I would most likely not have discovered that he was a fellow runner. We would not have connected with one another in such a significant way and an opportunity to alleviate his suffering without additional medications might never have presented itself.

Inside his home, surrounded by his precious belongings, I could see deeply into Brian as a person. His life history was on display for me, tangible and accessible. I have had many similar experiences while meeting with other patients in their own homes. Hearts reach out and connections are made within the safety of home. There is no better setting in which to offer loving, healing care to another.

23

LOVE NEEDS NO WORDS

As a writer and storyteller I have always had a love affair with words. My two favorite books are my dictionary and thesaurus and I have been known to blissfully while away hours of free time working the Sunday New York Times crossword puzzle. Words ... complete me. They are my companions when I am lonely, my inspiration when I despair, and my weapons when I rage.

But words are the tools of the brain, particularly the left hemisphere. And in their concrete and rational functioning, words are sometimes inadequate to express that which is intangible and deep – like love. There are simply times, as in the story that follows, when brain-crafted words must bow down to the ineffable power of heart-spun love:

Imagine the frustration experienced by a stroke patient whose left-brain has been so damaged that she has lost the ability to use words for communication. Dorothy was one such stroke patient in the nursing home where I worked, who was unable to speak more than these three words: "Yes," "no," and "okay."

While she could understand words that were spoken to her

and could formulate a response in her mind, Dorothy's brain was unable to choose the appropriate words to convey that response. When Dorothy did try to speak she could produce only a meaningless stream of gibberish, punctuated with an occasional yes or no or okay.

Yet somehow Dorothy managed to cope with this tremendous challenge and function with a sense of humor. On our first visit together when I introduced myself as her new doctor she frowned and kept repeating, "No, no, no." She reached for the notebook of pictures she relied upon to help her communicate and showed me the image labeled "Doctor" – a male figure in a white coat with a stethoscope around his neck. Again she repeated adamantly, "No, no, no."

I didn't understand what Dorothy was trying to tell me until our next visit. With eyes twinkling she opened her notebook to the same page she had shown me before. There she had used a pencil to draw some scribbles of long hair on the "Doctor" image so it would look more like me - a *woman* doctor. She laughed and squeezed my hand saying, "Yes ... okay, okay" and I recognized then just how well Dorothy's mind was functioning inside the wordless prison of her damaged brain. I also learned that deep connections can be formed even in the absence of words.

A few months later I was sitting at the nurses' station when James, a 46- year-old man with multiple sclerosis, wheeled his chair up to ask for something from the nurse. His MS was very advanced at that point and had affected the muscles of his face and mouth, making it difficult for him to speak clearly at times. On that day his speech was particularly garbled and the nurse could not figure out what he was trying to say. She kept repeating "I don't understand you" while James tried over and over again, in a louder and louder voice, to tell her what he needed.

As his frustration became unbearable, James began to cry

and pound his fist on the desk in a heartbreaking scene. At that moment the toll of living for years with MS, watching his body deteriorate and become functionless while his mind remained whole, finally reached a tipping point. James poured out all his pain and sorrow as the nurse and I could only stand by helplessly, unable to understand or comfort him.

Then from around the corner Dorothy appeared, pushing the wheel of her chair with her one good arm. She came up alongside James and reached out to him, gently patting his arm and shoulder with her hand, saying softly, "Okay ... okay ... okay." Gradually James stopped crying and leaned his head against Dorothy, the one person in the entire nursing home who understood exactly how he felt at that moment.

As I watched that beautiful scene unfold it became clear to me that words are often an inferior means of expressing the love that spontaneously emanates from the heart. Words, in fact, are like bandages we wrap around our brokenness, while genuine love, unaided by words, is the spark that initiates true healing.

As a writer and lover of words, it takes humility for me to recognize and deliver this message: my words are less important than the love I convey from my heart. And so, may you, and whatever brokenness you nurture within, receive the spark that I am sending, hidden within this wrapping of words. Nothing more needs to be said except, perhaps, "Okay ... okay ... okay."

24

SIXTY MILES TO PARADISE

It was late February when I first saw the poster advertising a three-day, 60-mile walk to support women with breast cancer. I knew instantly that this was a challenge I should take on. In the midst of a snowy winter, my workouts had dwindled and I needed an inspiration to start exercising again. I would have five months to train for the walk, which was scheduled for August. It seemed like the perfect thing to do from a fitness perspective, but I felt a deeper motivation, as well. My 36-year-old niece and a close friend were both battling breast cancer at that time and since each woman lived in a different state, there had been little opportunity for me to show my support. Training for and participating in that three-day walk would be a way for me to make a physical sacrifice on their behalf. I started my training and fundraising efforts immediately.

However, I began to experience some doubts about the activity right away. A few of my colleagues questioned why I would even bother walking. "Why not just donate money instead?" I couldn't explain to them why it felt so important to me to do the actual walking. And then, after the first week of training, I developed painful shin splints which interfered with my schedule and seemed to support the idea that it was foolish to put forth such effort, when raising money was the real objective.

But, as I hobbled along my walking path one day, still feeling twinges of pain from my lower legs, it occurred to me that the discomfort I was suffering was quite small compared to the pain I have seen women with breast cancer endure. I thought of all the patients I have encountered who have courageously faced mastectomy, chemotherapy, radiation and numerous complications, all in the effort to heal from breast cancer. They had no choice but to go through pain and suffering on that path.

Whatever small discomfort I was experiencing was my choice; I could stop at any time and just donate money as my colleagues had suggested. But, I knew that there was a compelling reason for me to dedicate myself to this training and the completion of the sixty miles. I knew there was something valuable to be learned, even though I couldn't quite express it or formulate it in my mind.

And, then, as often happens when I am walking or running out in nature, the answer came to me. I remembered once hearing a lecture about a Buddhist practice called tonglen, which focuses on breathing in the suffering of another and, through the exhalation, sending joy, relief or whatever might be needed by that person at that moment. One purpose of tonglen is to connect with suffering and cultivate compassion. I realized that I could practice tonglen during my walks, as a way to deepen my own experience and, perhaps, bring some form of relief to the women I was trying to support.

My plan was to begin every training session by thinking about each woman I was dedicating my walk to and focusing on her particular situation, breathing in any pain or suffering she might be enduring and breathing out peace and relief for her to feel instead. One by one I focused on my niece, my friend, and several patients I knew. Then I added another woman who recently came to my mind: the wife of an old friend of my husband, one of his mentors in medical school. She, too, was locked in a fierce battle with breast cancer, struggling to regain her health.

As my training progressed, my walks became longer and so, too, did the list of women for whom I was practicing tonglen. I would remember another woman I knew or would hear about someone else who was suffering and add her name to my roster. I was finding this practice very enjoyable. The miles seemed to fly by and I was never without something to focus my thoughts.

But, then, around mid-March, I began experiencing an unusual pain in my right hip— something I had never felt before. The pain mainly occurred while I was trying to sleep and, at times, would awaken me in the middle of the night. I assumed it was a result of my training, but I couldn't exactly understand what was wrong. In fact, the pain never happened while I was walking—only later in the day and usually when I was at rest. I spoke to a few of my physician friends who also could not diagnose the cause of my discomfort. My hip examination was totally normal and no movements of the joint would elicit the symptom. And so, I decided to just accept this mysterious pain. Since my walks were still enjoyable and free of symptoms, I didn't think I was causing myself harm, and I recognized that this hip pain could have other significance for me. My choice was to go with it and see what happened. After all, I had chosen to practice tonglen to deepen my own understanding of suffering. It made sense that I should encounter some pain along that path.

As I continued walking during the spring and early summer months, the pain gradually became deeper and more intense. I would lie awake some nights, unable to tolerate the weight of the sheet on my foot because it caused a sharp stabbing sensation in my hip. However, just as before, the pain disappeared during the day and could not be reproduced on any physical exam. I was even more convinced that this was suffering of a spiritual nature and I interpreted that I should practice tonglen even more intently when the pain was present. When I was unable to sleep, I would breathe in deeply, focusing on taking in even more pain and breathing out peace in a long, slow exhale. Surprisingly, I still enjoyed my training walks and felt well during the day. I could not explain what was happening, but I understood that the pain had a purpose and having that understanding made it tolerable.

Eventually, the weekend of the 60-mile walk arrived. Nearly 1,000 eager walkers gathered at the starting point to hear a kick-off speech by the race organizer. I was elated and filled with excitement that this long-anticipated event was finally taking place. Settling in on the 20-mile course, I found my pace and felt the joy of traveling by foot in beautiful weather side- by-side with so many dedicated walkers. It was clear that everyone else had come here, as well, with a sense of purpose. Many of the participants wore t-shirts bearing the names of women with breast cancer on whose behalf they were walking, some of whom had already died of the disease. Others wore pink baseball caps, designating them as breast cancer survivors, walking to celebrate the fact that they were healthy enough to take on this 60-mile course.

It was an amazing sight: a long line of walkers that seemed to go on forever into the distance before me and behind me, as well. I passed group after group of women and men who were singing or chanting marching songs, carrying posters, and dressed in imaginative pink costumes; we were, to a person, on a joyous mission. That night, I went to bed in my tent full of a sense of accomplishment and satisfaction for having completed one-third of the journey. As usual, my hip pain returned when I attempted to fall asleep, but after experiencing it for so many months, the pain had become part of my routine. I propped my right leg up on my backpack, trying to find a position that would allow me to sleep for a few hours before the next day's much anticipated adventure.

However, the second day of the walk arrived with blazing hot temperatures and a cloudless sky. Dehydration became a serious issue for all of the walkers as we pressed on through the searing sunlight over pavement that reflected heat of 120 degrees Fahrenheit. We consumed countless bottles of water and Gatorade in an attempt to balance our fluids, but still, many walkers ended up in the medical tent receiving IV solutions. The relentless heat gradually wore us down and there were no more cheerful greetings or marching songs heard amongst the weary participants. Pink costumes were bedraggled now; posters lay abandoned on the side of the road. We dragged ourselves over each mile, our legs swelling with edema and blisters from heat rash, exhaustion bearing down upon us. We were in the middle of our long journey, where reality erases illusion, unable to see light at the beginning or the end of this dark tunnel, uncertain when the agony would end.

As we entered the next town, I felt despair overtake me. I was questioning every aspect of this event and why I had chosen to be there. Nothing made sense to me at that point and I longed to be the kind of pragmatic person who could give up on something that was not going well and just quit this walk once and for all. But, that was not an option for me. I knew I could never allow myself to drop out as long as I was capable of taking one more step. And so, I was doomed to carry on in this misery. I had lost all sight of a higher purpose or meaning for this suffering. Placing one foot in front of the other over and over again, I stared at the pavement before me, numb and dull in the grip of dehydration and heat exhaustion.

But then, completely unexpectedly, I felt a few drops of cool water on my skin. Startled from my daze, I looked up to recognize that we had entered into a residential area. We were walking past a yard with lush green grass where two young boys were playfully spraying water from a hose onto us weary travelers as we passed by. It was a miracle! That brief reprieve from the heat was lifesaving and I felt myself surfacing again, able to think a little and pay attention to my surroundings once more.

On the very next block, with about a mile left in the journey for that day, I saw a woman sitting on a lawn chair in a driveway across the street. She was pale and emaciated, wearing a bandana to cover her bald head. She leaned back in the chair, barely able to hold herself up, but she was there to greet us as we walked past. I looked toward her and her eyes met mine, locking me in to her transcendent gaze. As she weakly raised one hand from the arm of her chair, she mouthed the words, "Thank you." I was instantly slain by this experience and burst into tears, understanding, once again, exactly why I was doing this, why I was enduring this pain.

On the next street, a man held up a crudely lettered poster, bearing a photograph of a beautiful young woman. The sign read, "Thank you for giving my daughters hope. Their mother died of breast cancer." He was weeping as he held that sign high for all of us to read. My heart was broken open. I was emotionally undone, but suddenly I knew I had plenty of physical energy for all the remaining miles. It was so clear. It was so simple. It was about the journey: a journey of suffering on behalf of all who suffer, on behalf of all mankind. Bearing up under the load we have been given, enduring and persevering against all odds, breathing in the pain and breathing out peace: this is why we came.

From that moment on, though my body was broken down, sunburned, blistered, and parched, my energy and purpose for the walk were renewed. I barely slept again that night with the hip pain, but I knew it was part of the plan, a key to the journey. On the final day of the walk I felt calm and serene, knowing I could finish the 60 miles and knowing, beyond all doubt, it was the right thing to do.

That last day I walked for a few miles with an African-American man, a minister who told me he was walking for his mother, the beautiful woman who had given him life. And he was also walking on behalf of all the other men who were unable to be there to honor their own mothers.

After we separated, I passed by two women who were abandoning the walk, sobbing with disappointment that they were unable to finish. And I understood that sometimes the journey doesn't allow us to finish— sometimes the lesson is in the leaving, no matter how much it disappoints us. I wished for peace for those two women, that they would forgive themselves for this outcome to their struggle; that they would know that it was meant to be.

The next rest stop we reached was decorated with palm trees made of cardboard and crepe paper and a banner that said "Welcome to Paradise." Some of the walkers joked with the volunteers, saying "You seriously think this is Paradise?" But, I realized that the journey itself really is Paradise, even though it entails suffering and sacrifice. Perhaps we just don't understand the definition of spiritual paradise and, therefore, never recognize when it surrounds us.

Further along the walk that day, I came across a heavy-set woman who was limping in pain. She was wearing a t-shirt with a picture of her mother on the back. Looking down I noticed that she was walking without shoes, her feet covered with painful blisters. I started to reach out to her with concern, but when she turned toward me, I saw a look of courage, determination and resolve on her face. She did not need my sympathy or support. She was fiercely on her path and knew it with every cell of her being. I simply nodded toward her and she nodded back, each acknowledging a fellow traveler in paradise.

At the final rest stop before the conclusion of the journey, the volunteers all wore angel wings as they handed out snacks and water bottles. I heard one of them saying, with certainty, to each and every walker: "You're going to make it." I understood that this journey will never be easy, but the encouragement and inspiration we need will be woven into the path, if only we are able to perceive it.

Finally, the end of the walk arrived with an enormous sense of relief and accomplishment. I took off my shoes, changed my shirt and doused myself with water. I sat in the cool shade for awhile until I felt inspired to watch the other walkers as they arrived at that finish line. I stood in a group of onlookers, lining the path and cheering. There was the minister who was walking to honor his mother! He cried unabashedly as he completed his journey, at last. So many people whose paths had crossed with mine over the past three days, walkers and volunteers alike, now streamed into the holding area. We were one massive family who had just completed an amazing journey together. All of them felt so familiar to me though I had never met them. We were strangers, but of one heart that day.

The number of walkers approaching the field had diminished as the event wound to a close. But I stayed on the sideline, surveying the last few stragglers making their way home. Finally, I saw her: the woman with bare feet! I knew she would do it; I knew she could finish. Her face, now stained with tears, still bore the determination I had seen earlier in the day—a look that would come to mind many times over the following years, reminding me what it takes to complete this journey in paradise.

Over the next few days after the walk, my hip pain gradually subsided, disappearing as mysteriously as it had begun. I thought I understood what it represented: that it was my crucible of suffering, given to me to deepen the experience of this walk, to teach me greater compassion. But a few days later, my husband received a phone call from his old friend, his mentor in medical school. His wife had just died of the breast cancer she had been fighting. He told us that the cancer had spread and become unresponsive to treatment. He went on to say that doctors had found a metastasis to the bone of her right hip in mid-March. She experienced excruciating pain in that hip for just three days and then the pain had suddenly vanished. Her doctors were amazed and could not explain it, but they were grateful that she lived her final months with relatively little pain. She had been able to enjoy the company of her children and grandchildren in those last days with peace and relief.

I now know that as travelers on this planet, each on our own uncharted and unfathomable path, we are all connected. We are each a part of every other being, sharing the suffering that is inherent on this journey. And I know that each of us possesses the capacity to lighten the burden for others, to help them reach their destination. This breathing in of the agony of life and breathing out the solace of peace is one of the ways we can be of assistance to others and to ourselves through this passage. It will require all the determination and courage we can muster, and we will be pushed to the utter limit of our fortitude. But, we will find what we need along the way: a few sprinkles of cool water, a smile of gratitude, and perhaps an angel or two to whisper words of encouragement.

You see, this, I learned, is truly paradise: to embrace all the suffering you have been given; to proceed along the path before you, no matter how treacherous; and to celebrate, with gratitude, that we are all connected in this divine and perfect journey of life and death.

PART VII

UNEARTH THE TRUTH

25

UNEARTH THE TRUTH

"And I felt like my heart had been so thoroughly and irreparably broken that there could be no real joy again, that at best there might eventually be a little contentment. Everyone wanted me to get help and rejoin life, pick up the pieces and move on, and I tried to, I wanted to, but I just had to lie in the mud with my arms wrapped around myself, eyes closed, grieving, until I didn't have to anymore."

— ANNE LAMOTT

At last, having learned all the earlier lessons of meaning, Divine sight, and compassion, you are ready to return to the traumatic experience you are trying to heal. Now, you can revisit that moment, bringing with you all the tools you have mastered, and look once again at each occurrence surrounding that fateful event. You are now capable of seeing the Truth in a way you could not perceive in the past. Now, you will have clarity and perspective that were missing for you in the early stages of your grief. At last, healing is possible and you will begin to detect it stirring within your soul.

∼

Finally on my journey I was able to write honestly and openly about my father's suicide. Finally I could look at all the details and feel the entire spectrum of emotions that had been swirling within me for so many years. Guilt, anger, confusion, betrayal, and shame all surfaced and emerged in my writing with intensity. I understood why I had kept them hidden for so many years—I hadn't been strong enough to carry so much pain out in the open. But writing was my salvation as I finally released the emotions and reflected on them, which became the next part of the journey.

You too will need to become strong before you can explore the depths of your feelings. The night may seem to get darker for a time as repressed emotions come to light and you may need to "lie in the mud" as Anne Lamott wrote until you don't have to anymore. But write it all down when you are able.

Writing Prompts

1. What parts of your story have you been afraid to tell?
2. What emotions need to come to light?
3. How does it feel to write honestly about the past?

26

MEADOWLARK

For months the words would echo through my head and haunt my fitful, troubled sleep. Countless times a day I would relive that moment: holding the telephone receiver to my ear and hearing my brother say the words that changed my life in an instant: "Dad died today." Upon that first hearing I was frozen ... numb ... dizzy ...with a buzzing in my head like that emitted by a fading fluorescent light. I heard pieces of the story ... "a gun" ... "the garage" ... "blood" ...

"Mom screaming" ... "the neighbors" ... "the police" ... But the entire time my brother spoke, I concentrated on trying to wake up—to feel the warmth of my comforter over my shoulders, the softness of my pillow cradling my head: those familiar reassurances that this was only a dream. But the tears in my husband's eyes, the somber and concerned faces of my staff, the hushed and suspended activity of the normally bustling office, all served to jar me to reality.

Dad was gone. He took his own life with a .357 Magnum pistol from his gun collection while Mom was out shopping. He chose the dark, overstuffed, dingy garage, full of boxes and boxes of our family memories, as the place to come to an end.

Every moment of his entire life—every tear, every smile, every sunrise, every held hand, every raindrop, every breeze, every leaf—had conspired together to bring him to that final moment: that last breath, last blink of an eye, last swallow of saliva, last twitch of a thumb. Everything terminated with the motion of the steel firing pin and the propulsion of a single bullet through flesh, bone, space, time. Silence. Everything at an end.

And then the rain came. For three days we rushed under umbrellas to the church, the mortuary, homes of friends and relatives; dodging lightning bolts which slashed the black sky, mixing our tears with raindrops until we were soaked with our grief. Wringing out over and over again the water of the sky, of his life, of our sadness; we were never dry. The sky burst open. Heaven wept. He was gone. Mourners huddled under eaves with hoods covering their heads. Umbrellas dotted the cemetery with bright spots of color. Howling winds rivaled the minister's voice for our attention. We were battered, spent, emptied by the storm of grief.

But, the day after his body was laid in the ground—after dirt was shoveled over the casket that held his pieced-together remains—that day, the storm subsided. The rain stopped. A shy sun lingered behind high cirrus clouds, radiating lavish light and faint warmth on those of us below. Peace. Relief. We sighed collectively with the earth, revering the power of Nature, grateful for this release from the storm's assault.

I visited Dad's grave that day with my four- month-old baby daughter sleeping in my arms, peacefully unaware of storms and grief. Dad was buried on a hillside overlooking the Platte River, surrounded by fields of grey-green sagebrush and prickly cactus. The wind, the perpetual Wyoming wind, blew the grasses into diagonal rows and the trees into a slanted stance, like a line of soldiers all tilting to salute the sky. Dad loved the wind. "It blows the bad weather away!" he would say.

I dug my fingers into the freshly turned dirt. I grabbed a handful of purple lupine and yellow coreopsis from the funeral arrangement that shrouded his grave and pressed them to my face. The fragrance carried me to our cabin in the Bighorn Mountains— Dad's special sanctuary he had built with his own hands. I wept.

Over and over I sobbed my mantra, "I'm sorry, Daddy. I'm sorry, Daddy."

Sorry for all of the unspoken words, the unbaked sour cream raisin pies, the undiscovered trails, the unobserved sunsets. This was my private rite of mourning in honor of those moments known only to the two of us.

"I'm sorry I couldn't save you, Daddy. I'm sorry. I'm sorry."

The tears and the words erupted from the deepest place inside of me. I couldn't stop them. I poured out my sorrow over his grave in such a torrent that it seemed to me the tears might tumble down the hillside and overflow the banks of the Platte. I did not know when it would end.

Grief following a suicide death is particularly poignant, accompanied by overwhelming guilt and the never-ending search for a reason why. Everyone close to the departed wonders if something could or should have been done to prevent this. Each survivor asks difficult questions about the tragedy and feels somehow to blame for not intervening or recognizing the signs or saying just the right thing. I was especially devastated by guilt because I am a physician and I routinely treat depression. I am supposed to save lives—that was the purpose for all my years of training and hard work. How could I fail to save the life of someone who mattered so much to me? How could I go on living knowing that I had failed my father? How could I ever practice medicine again?

I would not know that day on the hillside overlooking the Platte River, just how long the pain of grief would last, just how many times I would review the same questions over the next years of my life, and just how much my own future would be shaped by the oppressive anguish that had overtaken my soul. For, I was only at the beginning of a dark and dangerous journey. This flood of tears would wash me away to drift for a seeming eternity on a sea without a shore, under a night sky without stars.

But on that day, when it seemed there could be no end to my crying, unexpectedly, my sobs were interrupted by a sound —a sound that I realized had actually been present since my arrival at the gravesite. A sound that beckoned my memory and demanded my attention. It was the song of a meadowlark. And there he sat, perched on a barbed wire fence directly in front of me. His bright yellow breast glistening in the sun. Head raised to the sky. Singing his song over and over and over again. The song was at once a requiem for my father, a lullaby for my baby daughter, and a reveille for my mournful soul.

You see, meadowlarks abound in the shared memories of my father and me. The meadowlark is the State Bird of Wyoming and, like my father, loves wide-open spaces, which are common in our state. Irrigating pastures, horseback riding in the corral, fishing Spring Creek, picnicking on Casper Mountain, wading in Alcova Lake, relaxing on the deck of the cabin—all these activities were accompanied by the sweet, melodious voice of the meadowlark. Dad loved the meadowlark's song and always pointed it out to me whenever one of the birds was nearby.

Ornithologists use phonetics to mimic bird songs and help them remember the pitch, melody, and rhythm of each bird species' unique vocalizations. The lilting song of the meadowlark has been described by some experts as saying: "Oh, yes, I am a pretty little bird..." But that day, in the cemetery, the meadowlark's persistent song spoke to me:

"Hold on, everything will be all right; everything will be all right."

Now, this meadowlark, such a powerful symbol of my relationship with my father, attended me in my sorrow, harmonizing with my cry of lament, transporting me through time. He stayed with me throughout my graveside ritual that lasted much of the afternoon. Though I stared at him and moved closer to his perch on the fence, he did not move. There was never once a pause in his singing. As my tears gradually ceased and peace began to fill the drained reservoirs of my soul, he continued to sing, inspiring me with his steadfastness and perseverance. "Hold on, everything will be all right." Eventually, I was able to say goodbye to my father that day, and turn to leave the cemetery, clutching a handful of lupine as a keepsake, with the meadowlark's song fading into the distance.

A few months later, I made the 90-mile drive over dusty, rutted roads through the Bighorn Mountains to return to Dad's cabin. It was my first trip there since his death, and I was hesitant to plunge back into the pain I knew I would feel there. But as I stepped from the deck of the cabin to the lupine meadow out back, my heart soared. A smile graced my lips when I heard the song. "Hold on, everything will be all right." A meadowlark perched on the fence. Singing my father's melody in the land of his heart. He is not gone. We will not forget.

The memory of that song, and the bird that stood by me so faithfully on that difficult day, would become a lifeline for me during the years I drifted on the sea of grief. When washed overboard by a deluge of sorrow, I would grab ahold and somehow stay afloat. When marooned by loneliness and isolation, I would hoist myself hand over hand, back to safer waters.

I had questioned on that day whether I could continue to be a doctor after this devastation. The answer was, "No." I could not continue to be the same doctor I had been before my father's death. Nothing would ever be the same again once I began that uncharted voyage of loss. But a transformation was occurring that I could not predict on that day in the cemetery.

Shattered by my father's death, my heart would become capable of absorbing pain as great as the ocean I floundered upon; and my vision would be sharpened to pierce the darkness and see the tiny flickering light of a lost soul in the distance. I was becoming a doctor who could ask a patient, "Why you?" and who could see the Divine inside every person, no matter how distressing the disguise. Most importantly, I was learning to impart, with steadfastness and perseverance the simple guidance that had salvaged me:

"Hold on, everything will be all right; everything will be all right."

27

SHATTERED

With one bullet
a lifetime
of pain
is shattered into thousands of tiny fragments that
    silently shower your survivors.
Pointed shards of life:exploded pierce to the heart
    releasing
pain ...
more pain ... more pain ... tumbling like dominoes.
Did you know,
with cold steel pressed to hard palate,
what would be undone?

PART VIII

CLEANSE THE SOUL

28

CLEANSE THE SOUL

"You will lose someone you can't live without, and your heart will be badly broken, and the bad news is that you never completely get over the loss of your beloved. But this is also the good news. They live forever in your broken heart that doesn't seal back up. And you come through. It's like having a broken leg that never heals perfectly—that still hurts when the weather gets cold, but you learn to dance with the limp."

— Anne Lamott

At this stage, with a newfound understanding of the trauma that you have experienced, you are free to begin purging yourself of the shame and guilt that have haunted you throughout the years. Seeing the truth of the past releases you from those chains you have imposed upon yourself and frees your soul to take flight and continue on its spiritual journey.

Like a puzzle that begins to take shape so that you can glimpse its whole image, my entire grief journey began to make sense to me after many years. My emotions no longer tortured me from deep within—they were now available for me to explore and write about. I could see love and meaning and forgiveness and healing through the true stories that were coming to me and throughout the story of my father and me. I was living with grief—as will always be the case—but somehow my grief was integrated into my being. It informed my view of the world and other people and inspired my compassion. I was healing. I was dancing with a limp.

When you feel your own grief beginning to make sense you may think that your work is done. But there is so much more to discover. This is the trip of a lifetime. You will continue to change and your way of seeing life will change as well. Keep writing and let your stories reflect all the insights you've gained, what you know now that you didn't see before, and where there might be room for growth.

Writing Prompts

1. How does guilt or shame hold you back from experiencing your life?
2. Where do you see threads of grief woven into your everyday life?
3. What makes sense to you now about your grief experience that you couldn't understand before?

29

A HINT OF OLD SPICE

I saw you today
for just a second ... a glimpse ... when I opened
    the door
to the old storage shed
back home.
There you were
with your Army duffel bag
and wool-lined sleeping bag
(it must have weighed forty pounds— remember when I
    took it on a Girl Scout camping trip and couldn't
    carry it myself?),
that funny little campstool
that folded itself up
if you sat on it wrong
(I never mastered it),
rows and rows of shotgun shells all neatly lined up
in cigar boxes.
Your hunting gear ...
ready for the next big fall elk-hunting expedition (don't
    forget the poker chips).

I know what made me see you there today ...
the smell ...
that blend of sage, red dirt, tobacco and gasoline
(with maybe a hint of Old Spice). That scent is you,
    Dad ... and I could still smell it after all these years.
I closed my eyes
and breathed you in.
But when I opened them again, you weren't there
    for me
to touch.
Instead, I touched
each item of yours
and dropped
silent tears
on the dust of time.

30

CAVE BATH

The sign read: "No Swimwear Allowed. Nude Bathing Only," which confirmed my worst fears. I was a guest at the Indian Springs Resort, which advertised "Geo-Thermal Caves" and "Healing Mineral Water." I was interested in entering the caves and soaking in the hot mineral water, but the required nudity was more than I had bargained for. I wasn't sure I could go through with this adventure. Still, I had already paid for my admission and to walk out now because of my modesty would seem even more humiliating. I asked the attendant in the locker room if I could at least wear my robe into the cave. "Oh sure," she chirped, "but it'll get soaking wet from all the moisture in there." Since I had forgotten a towel, my robe was my only means of drying off, so I reluctantly stripped down and tiptoed off to the cave as quickly as possible.

I had come to this resort for a three-day personal retreat, hoping to take advantage of the solitude and get a chapter written for a book I was writing. Involved with a medical practice, my husband, two children and a dog, my life at home was just too hectic to afford me any large segments of writing time, and I was weary of completing only single paragraphs every now and then. So, off I went for a private little writing vacation. But there was more to it than that. My choice of that place at that particular time, my determination to experience the healing waters there had to do with something much deeper.

I was entering the darkness of this cave to explore the darkness inside of me. I was carrying something within me that I could not seem to face in the light: unhealed grief over my father's death by suicide. I had been in denial that this grief was significant and tearing my life apart until one day my office manager looked at a photograph taken of me at my daughter's christening, one month before my father's death. "Oh look at you ... I haven't seen you smile like that since ...." She looked away and didn't finish the sentence, not wanting to remind me of my pain. But I knew then that somewhere, somehow I had to find that smile again.

When I first emerged into the dimly lit cave from the access tunnel, I thought I was alone because I could see no one from that vantage point. There was a long corridor with four alcoved pools arranged alternately along the sides, two with benches nearby for sitting or lying down outside the water. I knew from the brochure that each of the four pools grew progressively hotter as you made your way deeper into the cave. The idea was to proceed in order and gradually become accustomed to the heat. I slipped into the first pool, relieved to have my body somewhat hidden by the refracting water, enjoying the temperature, which felt like the average hot tub I had experienced in the past.

Then I became aware of women's voices further inside the cave. They were talking softly and I could not make out what they were saying. But I knew they had to be at the third pool because I could see numbers two and four from where I was sitting. I decided to stay submersed in the water of pool number one until they left. After all, they only had one pool to go—how long could it take? But, the musical voices continued on and on, and the women stayed put while I began to become impatient.

Eager to move on with this experience and ready for a change of scenery, I decided to shift to the second pool. After I quickly lowered myself into the significantly hotter water, I listened more closely to the other women in the cave and recognized that they were speaking Japanese. I could see their legs extending beyond the pool. No wonder they were staying so long, they weren't even in the water! Their voices were lilting and their conversation was frequently sprinkled with laughter.

For a moment I envied their camaraderie until I pictured myself sitting naked by a pool with some of my friends. Not likely! But now I had a dilemma—I was not willing to go into pool number three when other people were obviously using it. I was far too embarrassed to display my naked body in front of them. I figured, though, that I could walk swiftly to the last pool and hardly be noticed by the women, who were rapt in conversation. It would be OK, I reasoned, to skip one of the pools, and then I would be done with this whole ordeal.

But as I made my rapid approach to the fourth pool, one of the Japanese women interrupted her conversation to give me a warning: "Too hot!" I glanced back to see her look of concern as I lowered myself quickly into the scalding water. After a few seconds I jumped out of the pool, unable to tolerate the heat and the rush of blood to my head as my body tried to regulate its temperature. I landed dizzily next to the pool, facing the woman who had tried to warn me. She nodded kindly in my direction, giggling softly behind her hand at my foolishness.

Suddenly realizing that I was no longer hiding my body from these women, I felt instant shame along with lightheadedness as once again overwhelming heat rose to my head. I needed to lie down right away in order to regain my physical balance and to restore my emotional composure. Recognizing my plight, the woman kindly gestured toward the bench where her things were sitting. "Is OK!" she smiled at me, motioning for me to lie down across from her and her companions.

Fearing I might faint, I took her advice and crawled onto the bench. Staring at the ceiling, totally embarrassed by my predicament, I could see the women to my right in my peripheral vision. The one who had spoken to me had a very large, round body, "Like a female Sumo wrestler" I thought at first. But then, remembering her compassionate smile and kind generosity, I decided "Buddha Lady" was a more fitting nickname for her.

While I reposed on the tile bench, trying awkwardly to hide my naked body with my two hands, I watched from the side of my eye as Buddha Lady carefully bathed herself. She sat comfortably next to the pool, legs splayed before her, washing every square inch of her skin, gently lifting each roll of flesh and each pendulous breast. All the while she conversed casually with her friends, totally at ease with herself and her body.

Meanwhile, I was consumed with the shame of my nakedness and this exposure in front of strangers. I realized that what I was feeling was a heritage of my culture and my religious upbringing. But my shame was also a heritage of my personal history. Teenage acne had scarred my face and had scarred my psyche as well. I viewed all my skin as defective and repulsive.

Suddenly, lying next to these Japanese women, I felt small. Not small physically, but small in my lack of appreciation for my own body, in my scorn for the roll of fat around my midsection, my sagging breasts, and my flabby buttocks. How could I feel such self-hatred? Here, I had come into these caves to explore a deep issue, the impact of my father's suicide on my life, and I hadn't even given that subject one thought. I was obsessed with shame about my body and unable to go any deeper into myself.

"What must these women think of me," I wondered. "Poor American woman, she doesn't know how to bathe!"

When Buddha Lady arose to rinse off in a shower of cool water near the entrance of the cave, I realized that this was exactly what I needed to do in order to recover from my overheating. I followed after her, but was too timid to stand fully under the water's blast as she had demonstrated. So, I stood just outside the cold spray, splashing myself cautiously with cool drops. I decided then that I was going to stay in the cave. I was going to do what I had come there to do. I started over at the first pool and reclined on the bench there for a moment to ponder my deeper feelings.

I had chosen to come here on that particular day, because it was two days before the anniversary of my father's suicide. This had always been a difficult week for me every year, even though I couldn't really admit that to myself. It didn't seem right to still be suffering over a death that took place eleven years ago. So, I had been telling myself that I felt nothing, my grieving was complete, but inside of me remained a deep, dark hole.

Though I hadn't thought of it in advance, it was very fitting that I had chosen to visit a hot springs resort, for my father used to love to go to Washakie Hot Springs in Thermopolis, Wyoming when I was a little girl. We would drive there sometimes on Saturdays and soak in the hot mineral pool. It wasn't particularly my favorite place to go—the water was too hot for me to do much swimming—but I loved to see my father's enjoyment. He would lie back in the water, head tilted toward heaven, eyes softly closed, and become totally, completely relaxed. At no other time in my life with him did I see that look of pure pleasure on his face. He seemed to let go of everything that stressed him and caused him pain as he floated there in oblivion. Afterward we always went out for ice cream cones— lemon custard if we could find it anywhere.

I considered the fact that I had been so overwhelmed with shame for my body that I had not even given a thought to my father's death until now. But, I realized that my bodily shame was indeed connected with his suicide. He had so despised himself, his entire being, that he had ended his life. We shared this deep sense of shame and unworthiness. It was not a mistake that I had been led to experience those feelings.

At that moment I knew that I wanted more than anything to be in that cave, sweating, boiling and baking until I was dried up inside. Surrounded by all this moisture, I wanted to feel parched and thirsty. I wanted to long for life and joy, to experience the extremes of pain and pleasure once more, instead of the numbness and neutrality I had become accustomed to for so many years. I wanted to ache for the touch of my husband lying next to me and crave the softness of my children in my arms. I wanted to cry over the beauty of the sunset and laugh at the feel of the wind in my hair.

I went to the shower again and this time immersed my entire body in the cold spray, just as Buddha Lady had done. And then, following her example again, I plunged into the hot pool, floating on the water, letting my hair drift gently about my head, freed at last from the tight top-knot I had twisted upon my crown. I floated, head tilted toward heaven, eyes open wide, wanting to see everything now.

I thought of my father's suicide and the shame and stigma associated with such a death in our society. Again I realized that this shame was a legacy of our culture. To these Japanese women, suicide was something different, a death with honor, a death with meaning, a sacrifice of one life for the greater good of all other life. It was a choice that could be made in their culture, not only from the depths of despair, but also from the highest place of knowing. I wondered what these women would think if I told them that I was still trying to heal from my father's suicide. And I knew ... Buddha Lady would look at me with compassion on her face and love in her eyes. "Is OK," she would say with her slight smile, the Buddha smile.

On my next break from the water, while lying on the tile bench, I remembered a dream that had come to me the night before. I had been driving on a dirt road in the mountains when I came across one of my uncles, whose truck was stuck in a mud hole. He was in great despair, not knowing how he would ever get out. I reassured him that I had my father's pickup truck, with a winch on the front, and I would be able to get him out easily.

"Clint's truck!" he exclaimed, reverently, as if I had just offered to perform a miracle for him.

But then, tears came to both of our eyes as we remembered together that my father had died. I ran down the road to get the truck, still weeping in sorrow. In the next scene of my dream I was riding back to rescue my uncle in Dad's old, red Chevy pickup, with the winch on the front. But, this time I was the passenger and Dad was driving. I felt so secure knowing that he would help me pull my uncle's truck out of the mud.

Then I said to him, "You know, Dad, the funny thing is, every other road up here is totally dry. And that road only has one mud hole in it and he managed to drive right into it!"

I laughed, expecting him to join with me in mocking my uncle's foolishness. But, instead, he turned to me with a look of absolute compassion on his face and love in his eyes.

He said with a slight smile, a Buddha smile, "These roads can be pretty tricky sometimes."

Sitting in that dim cave, sweat dripping from every pore, melodic Japanese phrases echoing from rock walls, my mouth and throat parched with thirst, I saw that it was me trapped in that mud hole, the only damned mud hole on the entire mountain. And I knew my father was advising me to be kind and compassionate with myself on this tricky road of grief and longing. And I knew, too, that while I carry my father's shame as a legacy, I also have his red Chevy truck with the winch on the front. I have the tools necessary to pull other people out of the mud. Now I have only to pull myself out.

As Buddha Lady and her friends walked out the door, I decided that it was also time for me to leave. I felt exhilarated, alive, and exhausted—excited that perhaps I was making some progress in this great task of growing spiritually. But, I knew also that this was just one bath on one day in one year of one human lifetime, in one era of this nation, in one eon of this planet, in one instant of this infinite universe. I knew that there was more work and more suffering and more thirst ahead. After all, I was scheduled for a 45-minute mud bath the next day. I couldn't wait to see if I would be able to pull myself out of that mud once and for all.

PART IX

BE AT PEACE

31
BE AT PEACE

"Someday you're gonna look back on this moment of your life as such a sweet time of grieving. You'll see that you were in mourning and your heart was broken, but your life was changing …"

— Elizabeth Gilbert

Finally, from a higher spiritual vantage point, you can find moments of sweetness where once only grief filled your soul. Now you have the capacity to interpret all of life's tragedies through this elevated awareness of the meaning and Divinity of life, the need for compassion toward all others, and the true mysteries of this existence. As you struggle with the paradox of striving for Life while surrendering to Death, you will, at last, see the path down the middle and there, find yourself at peace with the way things unfold.

Eventually I reached a place where my grief became my gift. I recognized that grief had given me new eyes to see the miracles of life and an open heart capable of carrying greater love. I wasn't finished with grief but grief was a cherished part of my life that had transformed everything.

Grief taught me how to live with its pain, which was enormously helpful when my mother grew older and faced her own end of life. Because of my previous grief experience I was able to reconcile with Mom, care for her during her last week of life, and grieve her death with much greater peace and equanimity than I could have imagined. And once again, writing provided me with the tool I needed throughout those years.

Ultimately gratitude has washed over me because I can now see the beauty within tragedy, the light within the darkness, and the vibration of life even within death. It has all become so clear. Everything I have written since this awakening has been from this vantage point. And there is still so much more to write …

When you awaken to see this "sweet time of grieving" you won't need this book or my stories or advice or prompts. You will be ready to share your wisdom and insights with the world. May you continue writing and growing. May your words change your life and illuminate every dark night you face in the future.

Writing Prompts

1. What brings you peace?
2. What do you see now that you couldn't see before?
3. How has your grief been a gift?

32

WHEN DOCTORS GRIEVE

I remember so clearly all of the idealistic optimism I felt at the beginning of medical school: the naïve certainty that I was going to help people and save their lives ... and I would do that through the power of love. Yes, I came to medicine with the awareness that love is actually the force that heals and I was determined to bring my knowledge of love to medical practice. It was going to be miraculous.

And I remember just as clearly the day when all of my idealism came crashing down around my feet, in my Waterloo moment, leaving me disillusioned and bereft. On that particular morning I was working in the Emergency Room as a 4th-year medical student when a trauma patient was brought in by ambulance.

She had been in an auto accident and had been ejected through the windshield because she wasn't wearing a seatbelt. We quickly learned that she was just 16-years old and had been on her way to school, driving her best friend in the car she had received for her birthday just a few months before.

She had massive injuries to her head and neck, and the ER trauma team moved in quickly to begin resuscitation. I was assigned to help with chest compressions, monitor IV fluids and stay out of everyone else's way. In a blur of urgent yet efficient activity, dozens of people worked on the girl, performing their roles in this well-choreographed death-defying dance.

I helped wherever I was needed and watched and waited … for the miracle to occur. We were going to save her. This incredible super-team of highly skilled technicians with an endless supply of catheters, wires, tubes, syringes, plasma, defibrillator paddles. She was only 16—just a few years younger than me. She would not die. We wouldn't let her go. I wouldn't let her go … I had love on my side after all. We just had to allow enough time for the miracle.

We worked on her for what seemed like an entire day, yet it may have been only an hour. One by one the technicians withdrew and left the little cubicle where the miracle was yet to take place. I stayed through everything, holding her hand, sending her all the love I could muster, believing … believing … she will not die.

But she did. The nurse removed all the tubing and wires and covered her lovely young face and curly blond, blood-caked hair with a clean sheet. We were giving up on the miracle. We were giving up on love.

I was devastated and broken apart—all of this intense, focused effort had been for just one purpose: to save her life. And now, just like that, we were giving up. I stood there speechless trying to comprehend what had gone wrong—did I not send enough love to her? Had I not believed strongly enough in the possibility of a miracle?

I wandered around the ER, trying to find someone to talk to about what had just happened, but the resident and attending were already working with other patients, the nurses were writing their notes and the orderlies were cleaning up, getting the cubicle ready for someone else. No one looked at me. No one noticed my pain. No one talked to me … ever …

about the death of that girl, or about the death of any patient.

I went home that night and fell on my bed, exhausted and numb. When I tried to kick my shoes off I found that, for some reason, they were stuck on my feet and I had to struggle to remove them. Then I looked inside and saw that they were filled with dried blood—the blood of the young girl had dripped down underneath the drape sheet while I held her hand, slowly filling my shoes without my awareness.

I crumpled onto the floor of my bedroom and sobbed and sobbed, holding onto those shoes that I would never wear again. I pictured the face of that beautiful girl, lying serenely on the gurney while her life slipped through our hands and her blood dripped into my shoes.

I understood in that moment for the first time the weight of the responsibility I was taking on my shoulders ... on my heart ... by becoming a doctor. The pain of losing that patient was overwhelming and the sorrow from the failed miracle was so immense it could drown me. I knew then that medicine would always be a life and death struggle ... for the patient ... and also for me. And I was no longer certain how it would turn out in the end. Miracles were suddenly hard to come by.

Many years later I was in a different hospital at 2 o'clock one morning, waiting for the elevator to take me upstairs to examine a baby that had just been born by C-section. As the doors opened I saw in the corner one of my colleagues, a prominent cardiovascular surgeon in our community, the original "Dr. McDreamy"--handsome, brilliant, cocky, rich, infallible.

But he was hunched over with his face in his hands, sobbing uncontrollably when I stepped inside. "Steve, are you okay?" I asked, wondering if some tragedy had struck his family. When he realized that he was no longer alone, Steve quickly straightened up and suppressed his sobs.

He told me he had just finished 7 hours in the operating room, trying to save a 29-year old woman who had come in with major chest trauma. He had done everything he could to repair the damage and save her life. But there had been no miracle. There was nothing to show for his dedication and perseverance that night.

I understood his feelings precisely in that moment. "I know," I said softly, "I know how it feels." We rode in silence, each bearing the pain of our own memories ... of so many heroic attempts and senseless losses. Of so many shattered miracles and broken beliefs.

There was little comfort for either of us in that moment as we each bore up under our pain, firmed our shoulders and looked straight ahead. Though we were both traveling through the path of grief, it was a solitary journey that no one, not even a colleague, could share. Then the doors opened and we each walked away to our own worlds. There were more patients to see ... more lives to touch ... more fragile miracles to breathe life into ... and to helplessly watch slip through our well-trained hands.

33
ANOTHER HOLLYHOCK MIRACLE

A few weeks ago I had the opportunity to attend my 40th highschool reunion back in my home town. I was a little apprehensive about seeing people from so long ago in my past, but it turned out to be a great experience. I was most interested by the fact that I now am able to find common bonds with some individuals who had seemed very different from me 40 years ago. Life has a way of smoothing out some of our ridges and knocking off our sharp edges until it reveals to us the hidden connections that were binding us together all along. Our conversations back in high school were focused on dreams and desires, while now, after 40 years of life's uncertainties, we spoke more humbly of loss, change and acceptance. We have travelled many diverse roads to arrive at this common destination.

During this visit, I took some time to sit my elderly mother, who is home-bound while she endures and embraces what I think of as the "slow days" of advanced age. Her world inside her home is very small now as she focuses all of her energy on simply surviving each of the days that remain for her. She sat in her chair patiently listening to my description of the reunion and tales of the busy, eventful lives of my family, all the while eager to tell me her latest news. Frankly, these days most of her stories get repeated many times over as she searches her fading memory for some small tidbit to share. But on that day, when she finally had a chance to talk, her eyes sparkled with excitement as she pointed past the kitchen window toward the fence that separates her yard from the sidestreet. "It's a hollyhock," she announced "growing right outside my fence!"

Sure enough, a single hollyhock stalk was growing there amid the weeds and tall grass, bearing white flowers, just like the picture on the front cover of my book. Mom hasn't grown hollyhocks for many decades and when she did they were in our back yard. And she hasn't been able to tend a garden or nurture a flower to bloom for several years - an activity she has dearly missed. But there on her fence, right where she can see it from her kitchen table, a single hollyhock blooms just for her. I imagine that flower is nourished by the prayers she continuously sends out for others and is watered by the tears she sheds over the inevitable pain of life. So she is still able, in her own special way, to work on her garden and see the fruits of her efforts.

If you have read the story *The Hollyhock Miracles* from *"7 Lessons for Living from the Dying"*, you will understand the significance of that hollyhock appearing there at this particular time. You will know why, to me, it is a miracle that deserves my awe and gratitude. You will recognize that somehow, some way, against all odds, life continues to give us what we need, even when our resources are dwindling and our days are fading. It will be clear that hidden connections exist between all of us that bind and draw us together at the perfect time, no matter how unlikely. And you will see that life's pain and uncertainties are really shaping us to be exactly who we have always been meant to be: smooth and worn around the edges, humbly accepting of loss and change.

34

BLESSED ARE THOSE WHO MOURN

On Good Friday I made my final visit to the house I grew up in, which has been sitting empty, for the first time in 60 years, since my Mother's death this past January. I have spent the last two months clearing out her possessions to prepare the house for a new owner. The work has been difficult but therapeutic, as I have agonized over her photos and papers and keepsakes – choosing which to save or donate and which to throw away.

After three trips back to my hometown the job is finally finished. The house has been emptied of everything except the functional furniture and I have closed the door for the last time.

As I walked away on Friday a heavy despair came upon me that I have not felt before during this grief process. The reality is settling in that I am ultimately alone in the world now. The parents who gave me life both are gone and even the house that sheltered my growth is no longer there for me.

. . .

I HAVE NO HOME.

Although I have my own family and house, I am still an orphan with no safe place to return to when life overwhelms me.

There is no door that is left always open for me ...

no light that burns in the window all night for me ...

no eye that sparkles at the mention of my name ...

no heart that has already forgiven my shortcomings before I even recognize them.

I AM IN MOURNING. I am finally beginning to understand what that means and to experience the depth and breadth of this process.

In his book "The Hidden Gospel" Neill Douglas-Klotz says that "to mourn" in Aramaic, which is the language Jesus spoke to the people when he recited the Beatitudes, can also mean "to be in confusion or turmoil, to wander, literally or figuratively."

Yes, I am in mourning. I am wandering alone and confused right now waiting to find my way back home – but home will never be the same for me.

It is clear that I must now make a new home for myself within my own heart. There I must create a door that is always open, a light that burns eternally, a spark that cherishes my name, and a blessing of continual self-forgiveness.

For the first time in my life I believe I now understand the message of Easter and the concept of resurrection. There is new life that follows grief and mourning. And I must continue to wander until I find my way to that place of comfort. This is indeed a sacred journey and though I cannot discern the path at this time, I know that I must trust it and keep moving forward one step at a time.

And I also know that there are many, many other

wanderers on this path of mourning, though I can't see them from where I sit right now. To each of you I send my love and compassion and a reminder that there is hope … there is resurrection. We simply must wait in the darkness a little longer before it will be revealed.

35
SOMETHING FROM NOTHING
A PATH THROUGH GRIEF

I recently marked the one-year anniversary of my mother's death. I was with her throughout the week before she passed away and had the privilege of shepherding her through that transition—a moment I had been preparing for since I first became a hospice physician. I knew many years ago that I would be with my Mom on the day she died and that it would be one of the most important days of my life.

Her death itself was actually joyful, though it was a process that took a great deal of inner work on her part, which has also been true for many of my hospice patients. Mom had been ready and waiting to "go home" for the previous 5 years and was relieved that her time had finally come. So as she took her last breaths I had to celebrate on her behalf, that her struggle was coming to an end, even while my heart was breaking as each thread of our physical connection slipped through my hands and I confronted the enormity of that loss.

For days after her death I was in a heightened state of consciousness—sensing her presence everywhere around me, exquisitely aware of the beauty and fragility of absolutely everything in existence. Every portal of my being was wide open and love poured freely into and out from my heart as I delicately negotiated those tender days.

But within a few weeks I had retreated into the protective cocoon of grief, while I went through the motions of daily life, numb and slightly dazed. I could no longer recall what it felt like to be in that incredible state of lightness I had experienced immediately after her death and I concluded that it had simply been a symptom of sleep deprivation.

Over the next few months I kept myself incredibly busy as I joined a mastermind group, traveled to a publicity summit, became a radio show host, produced a digital workshop and created an online interview series, along with doing speaking engagements in various parts of the country. I stayed constantly on the go and rarely took a moment off, even when I was "on vacation."

I was proud of myself for being so resilient and productive. I didn't realize that I had actually been hiding for all of those months from the grief that was mounting up inside me. But then everything fell apart: my radio show was cancelled, the interview series ended, my mastermind group moved on without me, my publicity contacts stopped communicating and I had run out of speaking engagements.

Winter weather had arrived, the holidays were looming, my calendar was empty and I had nothing to show for a year of exhausting over-commitment and frantic busy-ness. I suddenly recognized how short the days had become as I laid awake for hours in the darkness, lost in my own emptiness.

"This is my first holiday season without Mom," I thought to myself, remembering how much she loved these times of celebration and always made each moment feel so full … full of love and joy and laughter. And now, though I had the financial resources to buy anything I wanted or needed, I could not even begin to fill this emptiness that haunted me deep in the darkness.

How had she done it? What "magic" had she created to make each moment of anticipation before a special holiday feel so extraordinary, so full of meaning?

Searching for answers, I unpacked a box of some of her prized holiday decorations I had "inherited" after she died: a glittery ornament she and my grandmother had pieced together from old greeting cards; a tree-shaped wall hanging she and her sister made from broken green and brown glass (beer bottles my grandfather found in the trash behind a local dance hall) and adorned with old costume jewelry; various vases and candle holders she had crafted from discarded plastic bottles and glass jars, decorated with scraps of lace and fabric.

I had found these "treasures" of hers to be deeply embarrassing when I was a teenager and my friends from across town would visit our little house. They lived in huge homes, fancily decorated with porcelain figurines and hand-painted glass ornaments, which no one was allowed to touch. Yet my mother, oblivious of our humiliating low social status, proudly displayed her homemade trinkets as if they were priceless works of art.

Lost in these memories as I held the fragile greeting card ornament in my hands, I suddenly realized what my mother had been able to do all those years ago …

SHE HAD CREATED something from nothing …

SHE HAD EXCELLED at making each day seem special, even though her resources were limited. She managed to create little miracles everywhere she went, though her pocketbook was empty. She took things that were unwanted and discarded and gave them new purpose and meaning, finding the hidden beauty in everything.

She did this even with the destitute families she met who needed a place to live—she allowed them to move into the little rental house she owned, knowing they wouldn't be able to pay their rent for several months. "You will make it up later when things are going better," she would tell them. And her grateful tenants, relieved that someone finally saw something of value in them, almost always repaid her.

As I arranged my mother's treasures on a shelf in my living room, I suddenly knew what I needed to do. I would find my way through this grief that was smothering me by doing what Mom would do: make something from nothing.

That night when the sun went down and the temperature dropped well below freezing, I placed two buckets of water out in the snow. They froze around the perimeter and remained hollow inside, forming beautiful sparkling ice lanterns that later glowed with the light of the candles I placed in them.

I situated these ice lanterns at the top of my driveway, where they illuminated the path toward home in the deepest darkness of night though they were composed of "nothing" but water. Each evening as I trudged through the snow to light them I took comfort in the warmth emitted by those tiny flames and found hope that perhaps this light will also guide others who are wandering in the dark shrouds of grief toward the home they are seeking.

Though Mom will never again be with me physically and I will never again open a present from her on a special holiday, I have received the most important gift she could ever give me: the ability to cherish what really matters in life, to find the hidden beauty in everything, to make something from nothing.

And that has become my path through this process of grief: to continue to honor Mom's memory by offering up whatever I have as a gift to the Universe, free from self-judgment and embarrassment, cherishing each moment as a priceless work of art, creating always:

. . .

SOMETHING FROM NOTHING ...

LIGHT IN THE DARKNESS ...

FULLNESS WITHIN THE EMPTINESS.

IT IS ALL I can do right now ... and indeed ... all that needs to be done.

36

FALLING TREES

It's such a popular philosophical riddle, I'm sure you've heard it before. "If a tree falls in the woods and no one is there to hear it, does it still make a sound?" I remember when I was younger and first pondered that question. My response was something like, "Duh!" I would go on to say, "If a falling tree makes a sound when you are there to hear it, then, of course it would still make a sound if you're not there!"

I felt annoyed by the people who actually spent time thinking about this. I mean, who has that much extra time on their hands? Anyway, that was during my fiercely rational stage. I had recently jettisoned the religious dogma of my upbringing and was being trained to be a SCIENTIST, after all. How could I interpret the question any other way?

Many years later, however, that very query has come back to me, bringing with it memories and meaning that would have baffled my scientific self in those old days. It happened when I was out for a long run on a trail through the woods near my home. I traverse that path a few times a month during the summer as part of my exercise routine. On that particular day

I came upon a huge lodgepole pine that had recently fallen across the path, blocking the way of pedestrians and bikers.

As I scrambled to find a detour through the sagebrush and thistles, I wondered two things: did the tree make a sound when it fell? And, what caused the tree, which appeared to be living, to fall at that particular time?

Peering closely at the base of the tree, where the fatal fracture had occurred, I could see that the core of the trunk had been eaten away, rotted with disease that was not apparent in the tree's external features (at least, not to the untrained eye). But I could not explain which forces had come together at what precise moment to cause the actual toppling of the tree to the floor of the forest. Surely the diseased trunk had been slowly deteriorating for a number of years, gradually weakening the foundation of the tree little by little. But it remained standing until one exact instant in which the strength of that base was overcome by the power of gravity.

Did some other force assist in the process? Wind? The weight of a squirrel on one branch? The gentle touch of one human finger? Well, I will never know that answer. And, I had to conclude, at first, that it really didn't matter anyway. But, deeper into the woods as I continued running, some vivid memories began to come back to me.

Once, to celebrate our college graduation, a friend and I took a road trip to Yellowstone National Park. We were driving through a more isolated area of the park when we came upon a huge pine tree that had fallen across the road, completely obstructing traffic in both directions. We got out of the car to survey the situation as snow began to fall, an early warning of an oncoming Spring blizzard.

As we stood there helplessly (being in the days before cell phones), a crowd began to gather on both sides of the huge tree. More and more annoyed travelers were leaving their cars to determine what was holding things up. Each person reacted with the same jaw-dropping amazement to see the sight of this freshly fallen tree carcass blocking the path to their vacation plans.

As the group of powerless onlookers increased rapidly in size, I noticed that I could hear several different languages being spoken at once. Amid the now swirling snow I could recognize tourists of all races and ethnicities clustering together, gesturing and speaking loudly to try to overcome language barriers.

Eventually, it became obvious that we must try to move the tree out of the way. Hundreds of people lined both sides of the enormous tree and with an effort coordinated by universal hand signals, began to tug and pull at the massive obstacle. Slowly, inch by inch, we managed to move that tree out of the way to allow cars to pass once again, a feat which was truly remarkable.

The experience was surreal, from the blizzard bearing down and occasionally obscuring our vision, to this diverse collection of people that truly displayed the myriad possibilities of human evolution. All of us, united in one cause, with one effort, contributed to overcoming this, literally, massive obstacle. The event had astounded me and seemed to have the same effect on others.

We looked around us reverently at the newly unblocked roadway, fast being obliterated by snow, and hesitated for just a moment. It was difficult to leave after such a miraculous event. It felt like we should at least exchange names and addresses. But, the storm precluded any socializing and we reentered our vehicles and our private worlds, driving away from that shared roadway to our individual paths, never to gather again or accomplish another feat as a group.

That event stands out in my memory as a reminder of the power of the human spirit when many diverse individuals join together with a unified purpose. But, the image of that gigantic tree bringing traffic to a standstill on a remote thoroughfare also serves to humble me in the presence of Nature. The forces at work on the earth do not sway easily or bend to human will or logic. For all of our technological might, we are, perhaps, just pawns on the playing surface of this planet.

I was reminded once again of the sobering power of Nature several years later after our city appointed the first woman in its history to be Chief of the local fire department. This was a remarkable accomplishment for a young lady, just 36 years old, who was also a skilled outdoorswoman. Her picture graced the front page of our local paper as her fellow firefighters, dressed in full regalia, honored her for this achievement.

Exactly one week later, to the day, we would again open the newspaper to a full-page photograph of this same young woman. She had been driving home up a narrow canyon road to the cabin she shared with her dog, possibly reflecting on her first week as "The Chief". As she steered her pickup around a blind curve in the road, an enormous pine tree, more than 100 years old, fell onto the cab of the truck, killing her instantly.

That the tree fell with the precise timing and speed to land, not on the hood or the bed of her truck, but exactly on the cab where she was sitting, seems to belie the qualities of randomness and impartiality usually attributed to Nature. One second earlier or later, one inch to the right or left, and her life may have been spared.

Was it a breath of wind or the weight of a squirrel on one branch that finally triggered the fall of that tree? We will never know. And that unknowing is the source of our great anxiety and discomfort in the natural world. We are not privy to the secrets of Nature. We have been excluded from knowledge of the Grand Scheme that might help us make sense of such a pointless death.

The seeming absurdity of that event gradually faded into

my memory until several years later when another tragedy awakened again the questions I had been unable to resolve. A father, mother and their two-year-old daughter had been driving down a local interstate highway in the early morning hours, passing underneath an overpass that was being repaired. Inexplicably, an enormous steel beam fell from the structure above, landing on their car, killing all three of them instantly. Though there was other traffic on the highway that day and the beam was large enough to block all four lanes of the roadway, only the car carrying that small family was struck by the falling steel.

How was it possible that the beam fell with precisely the right timing and speed to strike only their car, sparing hundreds of other travelers that morning? In fact, my daughter and I were among the saved, having driven under that very overpass just thirty minutes earlier. While I felt fortunate and grateful to be alive that morning I could not ignore the fact that three others had not been given the same protection.

How could this have happened, and, more importantly, why? This unfathomable tragedy once again raised the obvious conclusion that Nature has no regard for individual human life; that we are the only living creatures on the planet who are not adapted to the order and laws of the natural world; that we stumble around this place barely cognizant of our own existence and totally unaware of any purpose for being here. And that, like unwelcome houseguests who have stayed too long, we would not be missed by Mother Nature if we were to disappear altogether. In fact at times, she unapologetically shoves us out and slams the door in our face at her own whim and pleasure, all to our great bewilderment.

These doubts and misgivings haunted me and brought back to my awareness the grief I had felt after my father's death many years earlier: the emptiness that had never been filled; the questions that had never been answered.

But, a few days after this accident, I had a dream that brought some light into the darkness of this mystery. In the dream, I was attending the funeral of the young family who had just been killed by the steel beam. We were seated in an enormous church and the priest conducting the service was posted at a lectern high above the congregation. Rather than pews, we were seated around hundreds of round tables, in groups of four or five.

As the funeral progressed, I realized that the priest was gesturing for me to come and read the eulogy. I was extremely uncomfortable and tried to hide, explaining to the people at my table that I didn't even know the family, I was only there as an observer and had nothing to read. But then, I looked more closely at those guests who were seated at my table: a father, mother and two-year-old daughter. Though I could see their physical features, they were composed entirely of light and their faces shone with love and happiness.

"Here," spoke the father as he shoved a piece of paper toward me, "we've written it for you. This is what we need you to tell them."

I understood then that I had been chosen by the departed to bring their message to their survivors, though I could not understand why. Ascending to the lectern, I opened the paper and began to read:

"To all the dear people who love us and miss us. Do not despair. When the forces of man and nature collude and collide to create such an incomprehensible event, do you not see the Hand of God at work? Do you not realize that every moment of that occurrence was perfect and just as it should have been? You cannot see the glories that we now can behold and you weep because we lost the only life you can perceive. But we are well and rest in perfect understanding that our paths were each fulfilled during our lifetimes. While you cannot know this truth, you must have faith that there is wisdom and order far beyond your ability to comprehend. For, this is the message we came to life to teach you and departed from life to help you remember."

I awoke from that dream trembling, with those powerful words etched in my memory forever. "Forces of man and nature", "collude and collide", "just as it should have been" .... I have pondered those words from my dream for the last few years and find myself no longer asking the same questions as before.

Quietly, I behold the trees that have fallen, the storms that have wreaked havoc, the irrationality of Nature, the unconsciousness of man, the collusions and collisions that have resulted in so many lives lost on this earth. I see now that I am blind, I know that I cannot comprehend, I recognize that nothing is familiar to me, I accept that I will never belong here. I may listen to the sound of a tree falling in the woods, but I do not hear it.

For this is neither the time, nor the place, nor the moment for that to occur. This is the moment for one breath, for a single heartbeat, for one blink of an eye, for the peaceful realization that everything, though perhaps senseless to my rational mind, is just as it should be. Everything ... is all right.

ABOUT THE AUTHOR

KAREN WYATT MD spent years as a doctor caring for patients in challenging settings, such as hospices, nursing homes and indigent clinics before she left medicine to pursue a new career as an author, speaker, and podcaster. She draws on her years of medical experience in the stories she includes in her narrative non-fiction books, which focus on the everyday spiritual lessons we all need to learn in order to live our best lives.

She is the host of the popular End-of-Life University Podcast and has inspired thousands of people to find love and joy in the midst of difficult times. Check out her website at
http://www.eoluniversity.com.

- facebook.com/kwyattmd
- twitter.com/spiritualmd
- instagram.com/kwyattmd
- youtube.com/eoluniversity
- linkedin.com/in/karen-wyatt-md-49723624
- patreon.com/eolu
- amazon.com/author/karenwyattmd

ALSO BY KAREN WYATT MD

7 Lessons for Living from the Dying
How to Nurture What Really Matters

The Journey from Ego to Soul
How to Transform Your Life When Everything Falls Apart

The Tao of Death
An Adaptation of the Tao Te Ching

Forthcoming:
Grief, Guilt and Gelato
A Journey of Sorrow & Joy Through Italy

Printed in Great Britain
by Amazon